The Fourth Magus

The Fourth Magus

A Litany of Personal Psychic Experiences

Hector M. Fernandez Jr.

Writers Club Press
San Jose New York Lincoln Shanghai

The Fourth Magus
A Litany of Personal Psychic Experiences

Writers Club Press
an imprint of iUniverse.com, Inc.

For information address:
iUniverse.com, Inc.
5220 S 16th, Ste. 200
Lincoln, NE 68512
www.iuniverse.com

ISBN: 0-595-19206-8

Printed in the United States of America

CONTENTS

PREFACE

One lazy summer afternoon when I was six years old, I felt so alone in the house because my parents went to the elementary school of the community to teach, my grandparents were upstairs taking an afternoon siesta and the house maid took my two year old sister to the neighbors for some diversion or gossip.

The house was unusually quiet in spite of the fact that outside, a tremendous amount of sunshine was enveloping the house.

"You can hear a pin drop," so they say because of the stillness within and outside the house. I looked around training my eyes on every single piece of object inside the house that I could lay my sight on.

I went to the living room, breezed through the dining room and stooped down in the kitchen when I saw a crumpled piece of red cellophane on the floor. I picked it up, tried to stretch it and then placed it over my two eyes as I remember some children do it some time back.

Wonder of wonders, it seemed I was in a totally different world. Everything had a tinge of red, even the sunlight. For some time I was mesmerized by what I saw and continued to bask in that scenery for a good half-hour until the maid with my sister arrived from the neighbors.

Two decades later, I would learn from the teachings of a spiritual school that I found that this world we live in, that we considered to be real, is but an illusion, a trick of the mind. That we, the people and everything that surround us in this planet and even the moons, stars and suns and the firmament itself are not real at all.

All the while, men believe that he is mortal but spiritual teachers say that on the contrary, men are immortal. They are not talking about man's physical body but rather of the spirit inhabiting that body, the spirit that animates man, as we know him.

The spirit is a spark of God, which uses a body in order to be able to express Itself in the physical realm.

There is also the consciousness that enables that spirit to be aware of what is happening in the physical world including the thoughts and feelings of the mind and the body.

Like almost everybody else, I have been aware of my physical surroundings as well as of my thoughts and feelings. However, I have had experiences that I know not everybody have had the chance or the privilege to go through.

I have written this book to describe those experiences. They may not be extraordinary to me but to people who have not experienced them, they may appear to be so. I don't consider them unusual because I know that people have experienced them at one time or another if there really is such a thing as time.

Some of the experiences I described occurred as dreams and I could swear they're almost real! But they are not; they're just dreams I saw in my mind, as I lay asleep.

The Teachers say that this physical world is just a thought in the Mind of God and once God stops thinking, everything will dissipate and go back to Nothingness, to the Reality that is God.

But is there really an entity called God, or is He just a pigment of my fertile imagination?

EARLY CHILDHOOD MEMORIES

My father will probably be in disbelief if I tell him that I still remember the events that happened to me from age two. He was surprised when I reminded him about a conversation we had some 35 years ago before I went into college. He said that I must have a splendid memory to remember events that he himself could no longer recall.

Well I do still clearly remember some of the major events that happened to me when I was still about two years old. For example, I could remember the old house with bamboo-slatted flooring and nipa roofing and sidings attached to bamboo frames that my grandparents own. My father, being the youngest among their children was supposed to inherit the house, being the tradition in the Philippines. He talked to my grandparents so he could demolish the house and replace it with a 1950's style two-story concrete and wood house. Since the old house had very hard apitong wooden posts (I remember seeing six of them) these were retained. However, the concrete foundations were replaced with taller ones to proportion the height of the ground floor with that of the second floor.

The old house was elevated about seven feet from the ground and one had to climb a stiff bamboo stair with bamboo handrails on both sides in order to get inside the house. Like most houses of old, it had three main functional areas. The living room that becomes a bedroom at night, the dining area that can also be a sleeping area and the kitchen cum bathroom. The space underneath the house serves as storage for unmilled palay, for farm tools and implements and as shaded areas for chickens to sleep at night.

The house was standing on the east portion of the lot about four meters from the road. On the west part of the lot as one goes down the bamboo stairs stood an old guava tree with very delicious fruit and near the gate by the road was growing an avocado tree with elongated fruits.

I do remember that as a child I was just starting to walk unsteadily when one time I awoke from slumber inside the second floor of the nipa house. Seeing no one around, I crawled towards the top of the stairs and started to climb down while holding on to the diagonal support of the stairs. I still could not reach the handrails. Halfway down, I lost my grip and fell down the stairs. I knew that I was crying loud but I could not remember if I have experienced pain at all. It was as if I was outside the body and just watching as the frail body fell to the ground.

When the new house was constructed, it was placed at the center of the lot but the distance of about four meters away from the road was maintained. I still remember there were many people working on the construction. I don't know where my parents and grandparents slept during the construction but I do remember that each night, they used to bring me to my Aunt Isabel's house located at the back of the property so I can sleep there side by side with her young children, my cousins.

When the house was finished, it had lots of capiz windows. Its walls were painted yellow while the wooden window grills and window frames were colored green. It was undoubtedly the most beautiful house in the barrio.

The ground floor of the house had different areas for various functions. It had a living room, a covered terrace, a dining room, a kitchen and a toilet/bathroom. The second floor had a family area and a master's bedroom for my parents. The four-poster bed of my grandparents was returned to the family area in the second floor. In addition my grandfather constructed a bamboo and nipa room at the back of the second floor over the kitchen in the ground floor. In summer, they sleep, cook and eat their meals there but during rainy days, they sleep in the family room by rolling out a buri mat. I don't know why but they seldom use the four-poster bed preferring instead to sleep on the floor covered with mat.

In front of the house grew that avocado tree which bore elongated fruits. (Actually the avocado is classified as a vegetable.) The old guava tree with delicious fruits had to go. In the meantime, some guava trees grew by the fence in front of the house. By the rear of the structure, the old "kamalig" or palay warehouse of my grandfather stood. All over the vacant portion of the lot grew some thirteen star apple trees bearing varied sizes of fruits, a jackfruit tree, some betel nut trees, a "pakiling" tree (its leaves were rough like sandpaper) and yes, a deep well at the rear of the yard which was no longer in use. By that time, we were drawing water from a water pump with a male-type pitcher located by the kitchen of the house.

Sometimes one can hear a thud down the wooden stairs. That would be me rolling down the stairs when I lose my grip on the handrails. These were events of my youth that were retained in my memory.

"Anda" And "Ima"

My paternal grandparents lived with us in the same house in Maronquillo. More appropriately, we lived with our grandparents in their Maronquillo house. My father was their youngest child and it was the custom in the Philippines that the ancestral house is bequeathed to the youngest. I still remember that the old house was made of nipa and bamboo except for the posts, which were of the hardwood, called api-tong. The roofing and the walls of the house were of nipa while the flooring and the stairs were of split bamboo.

In 1955, shortly after my sibling Girlie was born, the old house was replaced. I guess my parents took a loan from the Government Service Insurance System for the construction of the house. My parents were both working for the government as elementary public school teachers then. I must be about three years old then and I could still remember that I was usually entrusted each night to my Aunt Isabel whose family had a house at the rear of our lot. I used to sleep there together with my cousins while the house was being constructed.

I remember that all nipa and bamboo parts of the house were replaced with wood and cement. Whereas the old house had only an upper floor for domicile, the new one was a two-story house. The ground floor had a living room, an open terrace with roof, a dining room, kitchen, toilet/bath and most important of all, a water pump operated manually. On the other hand, the second floor had a family area and a bedroom. Since my grandparents really own the old house and the lot where it was standing, they retained their four poster bed at the second floor family area and a sturdy clothes cabinet called "aparador". There was a wide window at the back of the second floor

4

family area and what my grandpa did was to build a room on top of the ground floor kitchen made of bamboo and nipa. They still preferred living in the coolness of the native structure. They had a kerosene-fuelled stove called "kusinilla" which they use to cook their food and a low table for eating called "dulang". In short, the added structure served as kitchen and dining as well as sleeping area in the lazy afternoons. During the night, the old folks sleep on their four-poster bed in the family area.

I presume I was the favorite of the old couple at that time. Everybody said that I look very much like my grandfather, Apolinario or Tio Aryong, as his neighbors called him. I don't know how old my grandma Filomena was at that time I was three but I estimate my grandpa must have been about 74 years old at that time.

Whenever my parents would go to work, I usually come up to the "kubo" (nipa thatched house) of my grandparents to partake of their merienda (snacks) and of their lunch as well. My grandfather was very fond of smoking, yet instead of buying cigarettes, he usually prepares his own by slicing in thin fragments the tobacco leaves he harvested from his farm and rolling these in cigarette paper that he buys. On the other hand, my grandmother loves drinking Pepsi-Cola very much.

At times that I had the colds or bouts of asthma, my grandmother usually took care of me when my parents were away. There was one time, however, when I got extremely sick with whooping cough which was locally called "tuspirina". Initially, my parents would mix calamansi juice in a glass and leave it outside the house on top of a covered metal drum so it would get chilled with the morning dewdrops and I could drink in the early morning. My condition did not improve even after a couple of weeks, though.

My grandfather decided to take the next best step prescribed by the local folks for that illness; every morning at around three he would wake me up to bring me to the riverside which was about a kilometer away from our house. In order to get there taking the short cut, we had to walk a very narrow footpath with wild grasses growing on both sides. I was very much afraid of lizards and snakes that sometimes cross our path so my grandpa would usually pick me up and lodge me on his nape with both my legs dangling on his chest. I would then hold on to his forehead so I would not fall from my perch while he would hold both of my feet with his hands to secure me firmly. While he walked, he would ask me to look at the stars and the moon above, which were still clearly visible at that time. And so it was that I was introduced to the beauty of nature at night when the surroundings are quiet and the breeze touch the skin gently while the cicadas chirp and the lizards stir as they hear my grandpa's footsteps.

My grandma Filomena was an excellent storyteller. As I was growing up, she and my grandfather would usually sit face to face on coca-cola chairs (wrought iron chairs with circular wooden seats and chair-backs contoured like a coca-cola bottle) by the front window of the house right after they have taken dinner where they could see everyone passing by. They eat at the "kubo" part of the house while my parents, my sister and I eat at the ground floor dining room. I would hurriedly take my dinner and climb the wooden stairs right after washing my hands to whisk off the remaining rice stuck to my fingers.

On reaching the second floor, I would come close to my "ima" (a Pampango word for mother) and sit on her lap. As I was getting bigger, I would just coddle up to her standing rather than sit on her lap. At times, I would sit on the chair my "anda" (a Pampango word for father) usually occupy. Grandpa would then lie on the four-poster bed, propping his head with a couple of thick pillows and puffing his homemade cigarettes.

My grandmother would tell me stories about "duwendes","tiyanaks", "kapres", "tikbalangs", princesses, princes, sultans, kings and queens. "Duwendes" and "tiyanaks" are the local equivalent of elves and goblins; "kapres" are tobacco-puffing monsters living on top of trees; while "tikbalangs" are horse-headed giants.

I was always fascinated by the stories she narrated. I don't know if she made them up herself or she heard them from her elders. I'm sure she had not read them because I did not see her read anything. My grandpa could read but in the way a grade one pupil would read a word, that is, syllable by syllable.

The stories my "ima" would tell me catapulted my imagination to places beyond the community where we live but not really far. I could only imagine as far, and as much as I have seen, heard, felt, tasted, smelt, and experienced. My imagination could not soar beyond what passed through my senses previously.

Nevertheless, I was immensely inspired that there were places, wonderful places with mansions and palaces in surroundings much more beautiful than the place we grew up in and in my heart I desired to see and experience those places and meet those wonderful characters I've heard about. Never mind about the giants, "kapres" and "tikbalangs", I don't want to have anything to do with them.

MOONLIT NIGHTS

As I said, I had frequent bouts with asthma when I was quite young. My parents were both teaching in the elementary school so a younger sister and I were usually left under the care of a household help and/or my paternal grandparents.

I remember how difficult it was to breathe when one has asthma attacks and on several occasions I was wishing that I were "dead", literally dead. In fact, my grandmother admonished me for saying so.

Every time, the "pseudo doctor" of the barrio, Dr. Tiong (he was not really a licensed doctor but just learned the ropes through experience by assisting a real doctor), had to be called. He used to give me an injection on the buttocks or to make me take a tablet of medicine dissolved with water on a spoon which was really unpleasant to the taste. I had to be pinned down on the dining table by at least four persons before I could be injected with medicine or forced to take that bitter tablet dissolved in water.

Our house had only one bedroom at the second floor at that time. The window was shaped like an L with three capiz panels on each side. There were flower boxes enclosed with wooden grills. At night, my mother would usually lift me to the windowpane so I could watch the dark blue sky teeming with glittering stars.

When there was a full moon, she would teach me a short poem that goes...

> Moon, moon please drop me a bolo.
> What will you do with a bolo?
> I will use it to cut down bamboo stalks.
> What will you do with the bamboo stalks?
> I will make a ladder to reach you.

I was an unusually inquisitive child and would ask my mother where the stars and the moon came from. She would reply that those came from heaven. Then I would continue to ask where heaven came from and she would retort that it came from God. To which I would pursue," Where did God come from?" She would then admonish me to stop asking questions.

I would stop asking her questions but in my mind the questions would remain. I really wanted to know, where did God come from and whatever the source of God, where did that source come from and so on and on and on and on and on and on and on……….

I never realized that that line of questioning was the start of a search, my lifelong search for my SOURCE.

TREKKING TO ANGAT

Unlike my sisters, I, the first born of my parents, was born in Angat town, my mother's hometown. Angat town is some six kilometers away from the barrio of my father where all of my siblings were born.

Immediately after my father married my mother in the Catholic church of Angat, he brought my mother to his parents' home in the barrio of Maronquillo of the town of San Rafael, in the province of Bulacan.

A river separates the two towns known as the Angat River.

Old folks say that Maronquillo used to be part of Angat but due to the changes in the course of the river every time there was a big flood, it came to be part of San Rafael, the neighboring town. In fact, just across the river is a barrio called Marungko and it is part of the town of Angat. It is likely then that the name Maronquillo means little Marungko, having formerly been a part of that place.

My parents made it a point to visit my grandma in the town of Angat, every Sunday. However, there were times when my mother would decide to stay at home to supervise the maid with the laundry or cleaning of the house; when she would be ill; when she had just given birth to my siblings. In which case, she would prod my father to put me in a custom-made wooden seat in front of his bicycle so he can pedal on to Angat with me in front of the bicycle.

It was an ordinary bicycle with big wheels and my father was adept at riding on it. From our house in Maronquillo, he would pedal on to the next barrio called Pulo. At the mid part of that barrio, exactly in front of the barrio chapel is a feeder road leading to the Angat River. By the way, during the fifties, all houses were located alongside the main road such that when we make a right turn towards the river, there will be no more houses but instead the narrowing feeder road was flanked on both sides by assorted shrubs and trees.

Then about 300 meters further we will come upon a clearing planted to assorted vegetables depending on the season. We will then have to make a left turn to a footpath towards the landing point of the lone wooden banca that ferries people to and from the other side of the river. This was still a good 100 meters walk on dusty footpath with wild plants, shrubs and grasses growing on both sides. During the rainy season, the narrow road would be muddy so we usually cross the river through the next barrio of Angat called Binagbag.

The boat landing was at the foot of a steep hill. The wooden boat was very narrow with a bamboo balancer on one side (called "katig") and can take on about six passengers. My father would take my hand and guide me to step on the banca then he would come back for the bicycle and lift it unto the boat, holding onto it all the time that the boat was traveling across the river. I would cling on to his khaki pants in the meanwhile until the banca docks on the other side.

The passengers were usually quiet while the banca traverses the river as if in reverence to the entities that guard the river. On the other hand it could be due to the fact that that part of the river was so deep, one could not see the bottom unlike in other parts of the river that the shallowest part would only be just ankle deep, at most, waist deep. So everyone was careful not to utter a word for his breathing might tip the banca and drown everyone on it.

From the river on the other shore, we had to travel another half kilometer to get to the main road. Along the way, one would notice lots of "camachile" trees scattered all over the riverbanks. I love the fruit of that tree with its curled fruit, a little bit pungent to the taste but getting sweeter as it ripens and pops out of the skin covering it. From afar, one could see the Sierra Madre mountain range on the eastern direction from whence the waters of the river originated.

As soon as we get to the main road, my father would sometimes meet people he knew, perhaps acquaintances or sometimes relatives. They would inquire where we were bound and would look at me, sometimes trying to strike a conversation with me, actually baby talk.

From Marungko, the road was uphill because it leads to a place called "Taluktok" or apex of a hill. I loved the feel of the wind as it touches my face and my small limbs. I would enjoy the sight as we near the highest part of the road beside that hill because down below runs the snarling Angat river with its glistening water while from afar would be a better view of the Sierra Mountain range and up above will be the sky with its cotton white cumulus clouds hovering up above. I don't know how, but the sight never fails to give me a "high". Then it would be a descent towards the metal and concrete bridge signaling the entrance to the town proper. Angat was my first idea of civilization because it has a municipal hall, a public market, a public elementary school, a private high school, two cemeteries, one for Catholics and the other for non-Catholics (today, there is even a memorial park), a cockpit and most important of all, a majestic church with its patio.

As years went by, my father shied away from going to Angat except on important occasions such as All Saints' Day, Christmas and Holy Week. He was back to playing mahjong and cards with his friends in Maronquillo.

It was therefore my mother, and my siblings Girlie, Lerrie, and myself who would do the trekking to Angat. Emcel, Ethel and Erma would be born much later and I would be in Manila by then.

We preferred to pass via Binagbag during summer. From our house in Maronquillo, we would take a jeepney ride till we get to the chapel of Binagbag. From there we would take a long walk towards the river. The road was unpaved but not so dusty nor muddy because it was covered with big natural stones from the river. However, about 150 meters away, the road will slope down gradually until the river and the road was soft because it was simply earth. Therefore, we prefer taking the footpath, which was about six feet higher than the road to the river but running alongside it. The way was shady and cool unlike the feeder road of Pulo where the shrubs were low. In this case, the trees were tall and so the footpath to the river was pleasant. I particularly love the flowers of the flame tree when they were a-bloom. I usually strain my neck looking up just to gaze at those lovely red flowers interspersed with green leaves.

That particular tree gives me a "high"; I could feel it in my heart, an elation that I could not explain.

Then as we approach the river, we would know even if it were still beyond sight because we could hear its flow. This part of the river was shallow in summer, only knee-deep so instead of the wooden banca, we can just cross via the bamboo bridge that was constructed over the river for a fee equivalent to a banca ride.

From that point of the river, the way to the main road of Marungko was shorter but there won't be as many "camachile" trees as in the other way through Pulo.

I love nature and its elements, the earth, the sky, the river, the trees, the birds and the occasional lizards and snakes that cross our path.

But I would single out that flame tree in Binagbag, which used to give me a feeling of elation whenever I pass its shade with its beautiful red flowers. Could it be that the deity watching over that tree sees how I loved watching the beauty of that tree so it gave me that feeling of happiness? Or was it my senses that gave me that feeling of elation? Most of the time we take for granted our "five senses" yet without them, we would not experience the pains and joys of existing in the physical realm.

AN UNLIKELY PRESENCE

My maternal grandfather died in 1945 right after the Second World War of heart attack. My grandmother gave birth to her youngest daughter in June 1946. Auntie Nellie therefore, did not 1946 therefore, did not get to see her own father.

I did not get to see him, too. My mother eloped and got married with my father when she was seventeen. I was born three years later after my Aunt Nellie was born.

My maternal grandmother was the first born of her parents, my mother was the first born of her parents and I was the first born of my parents. Happily, I was able to see and got to be pampered by my great grandparents, my maternal grandmother's parents.

When I was ten years old, I lived with the remaining members of my maternal grandmother's family, that is, without my grandfather and my mother. One time, Inay Baning as we called her, packed all her children to Manila and bought an old wooden house there so she can send her children to Manila colleges and universities. My mother was not included because she already has her own family. In effect, I got to represent her in that matriarchal family. In fact, most people thought I was my widowed grandmother's youngest child.

I used to hear stories about my maternal grandfather from my grandma and her children as they reminisce about life in Cavite City, home to most American naval men where they lived for about four years before the outbreak of war. My grandfather used to work with the U.S. Navy as brass band conductor. My mother took after her father in musicality; she is a good piano player considering that as a child she took up piano lessons for one year only. My uncle Aguinal also took after my grandfather in that he could play the clarinet and in fact belonged to a brass band in Angat, Bulacan. Another Auntie, Tita Nene, the most beautiful among my grandmother's daughters, sing beautifully when she was still in the prime of her youth.

According to stories I heard, my grandfather, whose name was Alfonso Marcelo was a strict husband and father. He was not only strict; he used to slap or punch my grandmother at the slightest provocation, such as when he did not like the food on the table.

However, I guess he must have been a protective father because I heard that when they ran to the mountains during the Japanese occupation, he used to carry two pails hanging from a bamboo pole on his shoulder where two of his children ride.

He was also a devoted family man because he abandoned his post with the U.S. Navy when the war broke out to care for his family.

Before the war broke out, he was already able to construct a decent concrete house for his family in the town of Angat. He bought a piano for my mother, the eldest among his children and hired a tutor to teach her. She was only able to study her piano lessons for a year because the war broke out.

As I said, he did not report for duty during the war and the Japanese must have been suspicious because they used to go to my grandparents' house on the pretext that they wanted to hear my young mother, Erlinda, play the piano.

The concrete house was now gone, having been heavily damaged by bomb explosions before the war ended. In its stead was constructed a simple wooden house with corrugated galvanized iron roofing.

My mother had very good ear for music. With her limited music education, she could play any tune she hears. In fact, when I and my sister, Girlie, were taking up piano lessons, whenever we practice and our fingers press the wrong piano key, she would shout from the kitchen the right flat or sharp key to press.

I earlier mentioned that when my parents got married, they lived in my paternal grandparents' house in the neighboring town of San Rafael. The well-known Angat River separates the two towns. Our house in the barrio of Maronquillo is some six kilometers away from the town proper of Angat where my mother hailed and where I was also born.

When I was still five or six years old, I used to come up to my paternal grandparents' nipa room at the second floor of the house so I could be with them. My parents would be in school teaching in the morning and in the afternoon.

I used to watch my grandmother cook their lunch over the "kusinilya", a small kerosene stove. They had a low table, a "dulang" somewhat similar to the low tables that the Japanese use. We sit on the bamboo-slatted flooring and eat rice with fish or some meat and vegetables using our bare hands.

After lunch, my grandmother would advise me to lie down on the bamboo flooring by the window to take an afternoon siesta so I would grow fast.

She would usually hum a lullaby to lull me to sleep.

The roof of the room was of nipa as well as the walls. The floor was of bamboo-slats and surrounding the house were several star apple trees that sway their branches when the wind blows.

The main structure of the house was wood with corrugated galvanized iron for roofing. Yet, my grandfather opted to construct this room at the rear of the second floor by himself. It was the old folks' favorite spot. They would stay there most of the day. It is only at night when the climate is cooler that they will enter the main house to sleep on their four-poster bed. However, during summer months, they preferred sleeping in the nipa hut by rolling out a buri mat on the bamboo floor. I understand now their fondness for that room; it was perfectly cool even during summer months.

As soon as I fell asleep by the window of that room, I would be conscious of a presence, which I think envelops me, as if hugging me.

I felt as if I were shaped like an egg and a shell, an invisible shell was protecting me in my sleep.

I don't know how or why but I always thought about my maternal grandfather, Alfonso, whenever I felt that coziness. I felt protected and I know I felt tickled by the passing of the wind, too.

At that time, I have not heard yet about my departed grandfather. I didn't even know his name and yet **I know** deep within me that it was his presence that I felt.

Years later, I would learn from theosophists that people who had died linger on at the astral plane for a maximum of forty years. In the astral region, they can see, feel, hear and mingle with us who are in the physical plane. But we don't see or hear them. Could it be that though already dead, my grandfather witnessed my mother's marriage and he knew that I was his grandson?

A REINCARNATION STORY

Life in the barrio was so simple.

So simple that if you are not a farmer who has to do something in the fields early in the morning to pull out the weeds that could stunt the growth of your crops, watch over your cattle as they graze or get your animals from the fields if you left them there in the morning so you can give them water with some molasses to drink in the evening before turning in at night, you will find country life boring.

My parents were not farmers; they were teachers in the elementary grades.

My father did not want to be a farmer, he wanted to be an engineer but my grandparents could not afford to send him to college for an engineering degree so he settled for a course in teaching.

We did not have any field to till or cattle to tend. Once we had poultry of egg-laying chickens but that was when I was studying in college. Before that, when I was still very young, we had lots of doves and some turkeys. Eventually, the doves disappeared little by little. As for the turkeys, they were all roasted when there was a barrio fiesta that happens only once every three years.

We did have plenty of decorative plants to water in the morning or in the late afternoon. We had plants around the house and in flowerpots by the windows of the second floor. They bore beautiful flowers in pinks and yellows and kept the house fresh with the oxygen they breathe out.

Since I was not born to be a farmer's child, I did not have much to do when I was still young. In the afternoons, I had to find a way to keep me from being bored. One of the few diversions that we had was a weekly magazine called "Liwayway" (sunrise) published in the vernacular, which is Tagalog. Otherwise, from time to time, we get hold of some old issues of comics magazine, those illustrated magazines with varied stories.

One time, I went across the road to the corner store owned by Tia Leoncia Ingaran. The store was manned usually by Nene, her teenage daughter. Also living there was Tony, also a teenager. Though much older than I was, we used to exchange stories most of the time so I consider him as a friend. These two were siblings of Nello and Muding. The latter just set up house beside his mother's house, having just been married. But the three, Nello, Tony and Nene were still staying with their widowed mother.

There was a bamboo bench outside the store where customers can sit or while away the time while waiting to be served refreshments, if they ordered soft drinks and some bread.

There were no customers that afternoon, perhaps most people were taking a rest but I was not used to taking a nap in the afternoon. My parents have gone to the town to attend a teachers' meeting and I did not know what time they will be back. I saw Tony reading a comics magazine. It was a past issue. I hang around and when I noticed that he was through, I borrowed the comics from him. He handed it to me instantly and went inside the store.

I browsed through the pages of the comics, so eager to see the illustrations and the stories that I could read. My attention was particularly caught by the story about a dying holy man from the far away land of Tibet in a monastery high up in the snowy mountains. It was not the mystery of the land described that fascinated me, rather it was how the monks were able to find a child who in the story was said to be the reincarnation of the Dalai Lama. I read the story twice or maybe even thrice, taking note of the details of the death and birth of the spirit of the entity known as the Dalai Lama.

The story fascinated me no end. For years and years, I could not forget that story. Whenever I am alone, I would recall the story I read in the comics and daydream that I was the Dalai Lama. Then in my imagination I would concoct stories as to what sort of life I would like to lead in a faraway and fascinating land high up in the mountains.

My curiosity about reincarnation would not have been satisfied until I was 26 years old when I found a school teaching about the rationale for reincarnation and karma, its twin law. I will discuss about this in another book.

Unknowingly, the comics story opened for me the possibility of **man's immortality.**

THE FOURTH MAGUS

From the horizon, one could see the approaching figure of three men on horseback. As they drew nearer it could be discerned that they were no ordinary men but rather men of exceptional qualities. Yes, they were no other than the three Magi, the wise ones. I was on the street in front of our house in Barrio Maronquillo, town of San Rafael, province of Bulacan in the Philippines. The Magi were coming from the rice fields and I could see them coming into the community via the feeder road.

On reaching the main road, they stopped in front of Nello Ingaran's house, calling on him to come out and join them in their search. Nello was neither in the house nor in their backyard so I ran around looking for him at the same time calling out his name. I know that the three Magi were in hurry and no minute of their time must be wasted.

Finally, Nello heard my call and immediately approached the three men. He was told that they wanted him to be part of their team following the bright star. Nello saw the importance of their mission but he felt he wanted to say goodbye to his mother, Leoncia, in case he would be away for a long, long time.

He excitedly left to look for his mother who was not in the house at that time while the Magi waited impatiently on their horses. However, as time went by, the brilliant star was moving away fast. Fearing that they might lose the guiding star, the men told me to relay to Nello to just follow in the direction they will take. Then they hurriedly followed the star through the fields where they came from.

When Nello got back, I told him the message of the three Magi. So he rode his horse in haste and followed in the direction of the Magi. In the meantime, I tried to point out to him in which direction to go by running alongside his horse.

I was trying to help Nello find the Magi but either he could not understand what I was saying or he just could not see me. Eventually, I was left behind and I lost sight of Nello.

Unfortunately, after a long search for the Magi whom Nello wanted so much to join, he was unable to catch up with them.

Nello had been too pre-occupied with his search for the Magi and forgot that the real reason why the Magi invited him was to look for the child Jesus.

Tired and frustrated, Nello went back home a disappointed man.

I in the meantime wandered in their backyard and there found the scene of the crucifixion.

It turned out that had Nello focused his search for the child Jesus, he would have found Jesus in his own backyard as the crucified Christ.

I could hear footsteps, a lot of footsteps, somewhat similar to the stomping of the feet of cattle as they head towards a certain direction. I was very sleepy but the footsteps on the pebbled road of Angat town in Bulacan were disturbing my dreamy sleep.

Then I heard church bells peal. Suddenly I remembered it was the start of the nine-day midnight mass, a tradition widely observed by the Catholics in the Philippines in the observance of the coming Christmas Day.

I was already aware but I did not want to open my eyes. Then I heard the bells again and more footsteps passing by going in the direction of the church. I decided to open my eyes and realized I had a wonderful dream.

It was the 16th of December 1958 and I had just turned nine years old on December 13th.

I knew, simply knew that the fourth magus, **searcher of God**, was not Nello but I.

A CLEAR LESSON IN KARMA

I was nine years old, a Grade IV student, at the Maronquillo Elementary School, where my parents were both teaching, when the substitute teacher from the other side of town was assigned to take over the post of another teacher afflicted with throat cancer. It happened a long time ago and I don't recall the name of the teacher anymore but I remember her to be taller than my mother (who is 4' 11") and lankier. My mother was then teaching Grade II students while my father was handling Grade IV. He was therefore my teacher at that time.

Once in a while, the substitute teacher used to bring along her daughter at the school. I can't recall her name anymore so let us call her Marina. I guess she was a bit older than I was at that time, she was very fair complexioned, had a sweet melancholy face and long brownish hair. She would belong to the category of what Filipinos consider as mestiza (of mixed blood). She, however, had a distinct way of walking as if she would always stumble as she strode, her one leg being disproportionately smaller than the other one, a clear victim of polio.

It was the first time I've seen anyone gait like that and I suppose most of the people in our barrio seldom see such a manner of walking.

I could not forget that girl and I guess I never will for the rest of my life this lifetime. She had left an impression on me, a lesson imprinted in my memory that I never would forget.

As a child, I was very playful and very popular among the folks and among the students in that school, I suppose because my parents had been teachers of all the residents of that community who passed through that elementary school (at least those who were younger by ten years than they). Quite a number of my classmates tried to be very

23

friendly with me. Not only the guys but also the girls who at one occasion had the time of their lives running after me around the school grounds. I just donned my raincoat even when it was no longer drizzling and declared myself a Kapitan Kidlat (Captain Lightning), a local version of Superman when suddenly five girl classmates started chasing me around the campus.

The second time that Marina tagged along with her mother to the school, my mother invited them for lunch at our house, which was about half a kilometer away from the school. There was a short cut route at the back of the school grounds but since the teachers were well dressed and the fence to go over was quite high, we had to take the longer route, which was the main road. The main road was not yet cemented at that time; it was in fact very rough with lots of gravel to prevent it from getting muddy. It was summer at that time so the road was quite dusty. At the sound of the 12-noon bell, I went to my mother's room while she called out to the substitute teacher that we should go.

My mother and the substitute teacher started walking towards the road, the polio girl holding on to the right arm of her mother and her mother's dress. I could have walked side by side with my mother but I purposely allowed myself to fall behind so I could take a better look at the way Marina was limping. There was a train of students trailing behind the teachers and I could see the amusement evident in their eyes and their naughty grins. I know that the girl was feeling conscious, what with all the kids trailing behind her.

Then I started to be naughty myself. I started to mimic the way Marina walked to the greater amusement of the students trailing behind. I could see Marina's eyes glance toward me, she was aware that she was being made fun of by me. I did the mimicking several times to the restrained laughter of the other kids. The two ladies did not seem to mind or were probably playing deaf ears to what was going on behind them.

But I could see Marina to be so troubled by what was going on around her but she just kept her face to the front. I know that inside her, she was agonizing emotionally. Little by little the train of kids dwindled as they go home to their respective house for lunch. Halfway towards our house, I stopped mimicking Marina and walked beside my mother.

After that incident, Marina did not come with her mother to our school anymore.

As I mentioned earlier, I was the favorite of the folks and students of the place (at least that was my notion). Every recess time (one in the morning and one in the afternoon), we were always playing, running, jumping, etc. A couple of days after that mimicking incident, one of my father's godchildren who was then in Grade VI started playing with me during the afternoon recess.

His name was Arturo Valmocena with Turing as his nickname, a sturdy built boy who was definitely taller than me because I was unusually for my age. Perhaps I took after my mother in terms of height. He started playing with me by holding both my hands, asking me to step on one of his knees to serve as jumping board and then from there spring and jump as high as I could. It was fun, I tell you, it was really fun and I had a good time of my life. We were both laughing as were doing this routine when towards the ninth jump, my right foot hit the ground first and I suddenly felt a piercing pain. A pain which shot up from my heel up to my shoulders. I slumped on the ground, unable to stand. Turing tried to help me but I brushed him aside. I tried to stand up and pretended I could walk normally then proceeded to go up to our classroom nearby. The pain was getting excruciating as I tried to climb the stairs but I did my very best just to get to my assigned seat. I sat down and buried my face to my arms on top of the desk. The pain was getting intense and in no time, I fell asleep. When the classes resumed, I tried to wake myself up but my foot was really hurting. I pretended that nothing was wrong with me for fear that my father would lose his temper and hurt his godchild for what had happened to me.

Towards the late afternoon, I know I was already running a fever. We were usually dismissed at four p.m. so I waited till my father had stepped out of the classroom and most students had come out of the room before I started to walk toward the door. By then my right foot was swollen and each step that I made was a torture. Slowly, I climbed down the stairs, holding on to the railing, else I fall. Then I decided to trek the path towards the short cut. There were quite a number of my classmates who started to trail me as they noticed that something was unusual with the way I walked. Limping towards the shortcut, which means traversing the open school grounds, I slowly made my way towards the small feeder road at the back of the school. The students following me were staring at me and the way I walked. I know that some of them were smiling while the others felt pity for me as they see me grimace in pain with every step. They could not carry me because their sizes were just like my size. It was the longest half-kilometer that I had walked in my entire life.

When I finally reached home, I hurriedly went upstairs to seek out my grandparents, taking care not to be seen by any of my parents as I enter the house. There, under the care of my grandparents, I immediately fell asleep.

In the succeeding days, Turing brought a "manghihilot" (homegrown physical therapist) to remedy my swollen sprained foot.

I have not forgotten that incident with the girl with polio so when I heard and understood the Law of Karma, only then did I realize that I sprained my foot as a result of my mimicking the way the girl walked. Not only did my physical action bounced back to me, my emotions and mental state were affected as well, in the same intensity as I have inflicted pain on her emotions and mental state as well.

It took me 18 years to realize what had happened to me when I finally understood and accepted how the Karmic Law works.

MY EDUCATION IN MANILA

I studied at Maronquillo Elementary School for my primary schooling. At age ten, I was sent off to Manila for my intermediate schooling. In the Philippines grades one to four is primary grades while grades 5 and 6 are intermediate grades, both part of the elementary school curriculum. After that would be four years of secondary education.

In the summer of 1960, my maternal grandmother, Urbana A. Marcelo, a widow decided to send all her children to college education or at least vocational education for those who do not want to take up a college degree. She bought an old house at the most notorious district of Manila, called Tondo, locked her provincial house in Angat and packed all her unmarried children off to Manila. My mother was the only married child of Urbana or "Ka Baning", as her townmates would call her. In my mother's lieu, I was sent to live with my grandmother and her children. So at age ten, I was abruptly taken away from my childhood friends and transplanted to the fast paced life and tupsy turvy world called Manila.

I had a hard time adjusting to the standard of education in Manila primarily due to the fact that the mode of instruction was English whereas in the province I came from, the mode of instruction was basically Tagalog, the dialect in the region. We did have English subjects, though. Secondly, I was seated at the rear end of the room, second to the last row, such that I found it difficult to clearly understand what the teacher was saying. I had to trouble my seatmate a lot by asking him what the teacher said each time she spoke. That situation went on for about three months. I breezed through my grade five class as if I was in

27

a dream-like state. In any case, I was eventually able to adjust after a few months.

The name of that school was Lakandula Elementary School along Solis Street in Gagalangin, Tondo, Manila. Education in the city at that time under Mayor Antonio Villegas was free to all residents so one of my paternal relatives, who had long been a resident of Tecson Street, also in Gagalangin made it appear that I live with his family. Therefore, during the first two weeks of my stay in Manila, I used to stay with the Mendozas along Tecson Street. I love the Library of Lakandula Elementary School. It had so many books on stock. I've never seen so many books in my entire life at that time. I loved reading and usually frequented the Library during break time. I always brought home a book or two to read especially on weekends.

GRANDMA'S FAREWELL

My father came to school one morning during the latter part of the school year. He talked briefly with my homeroom teacher, Miss Bernabe, who then called me and allowed me to go with my father. My father just said, "We will go home!" That's all he said. I knew that something was wrong but he did not elaborate. We took a jeepney ride towards the provincial bus station in Divisoria, he bought a round floral wreath then we boarded the bus for the province. I knew that someone died, but I did not know who and he would not utter a word about it. When we reached home, there were so many people in the house. I was ushered into the second floor. There was a coffin by the west window. I wondered who it was on the coffin. As I approached the coffin to take a look, my grandfather who was seated by the north window facing the street turned around and saw me. He stood up and met me by the coffin. Together we viewed the remains of my "ima"; my storyteller had succumbed to a stroke.

My grandfather was crying, telling me that my grandma had already left us. I had mixed emotions as I stood there. I knew I should be sad but I was overcome more with excitement than sadness. I was excited because it was the first time that somebody died in our very house, it was my first experience of a wake for a dead member of the family.

So it was a premonition of death, that dream I had the previous night in my maternal grandmother's house as I slept. In Manila, there was only a single wooden bed which my uncle Roger use. The rest of us, uncle Aguinal and aunts Dely, Nene and Nellie sleep on buri mats spread on the wooden floor. I was still very young then, so I sleep with my grandma Baning on my left and aunt Nellie and Nene on my right. We use a big mat under a big mosquito net in the dining area.

That previous night, I had a sort of a dream. I saw "ima" floating on the air but I could not see the lower half of her body. She was looking at me as she breezed through while not far behind, my "anda" was running after her, calling out to her but she just flew away without looking back. I was shocked by what I saw and found myself seated on the mat gasping for breath. I could not sleep again after that. I was afraid I would see the other ghouls my grandma used to tell me stories about. Soon morning came and we hurriedly prepared for school. I forgot all about that dream I saw.

My aunt Isabel and my cousins were telling me after the funeral that "ima" was looking for me as she lay dying. Was I in her last thought when she died? According to Ka Nitoy, a spiritual teacher, a dying person's last thought is potent. If the person wanted to see a loved one before one succumbs to death, he would see that loved one no matter how far he may be located. He called it the **power of the last thought**. Is this what we normally consider as **premonition**, this kind of experience that I had. Did my "ima" really visit me before she died or was it just her thought that I perceived?

SCARED TO THE BONES

During the funeral march to the cemetery to bury my dead grand-mother, we rode in the jeep of one of my father's cousins. While we were following the hearse, my uncle would intermittently frighten me by say-ing that my dead grandma will visit me because I was her favorite grandchild. Besides, she was unable to talk to me before she died. I would brush aside his suggestion and refuse to listen to his frightening jokes.

After the funeral, we all went home, cleaned the house and pretended everything was back to normal. My father told me to sleep beside my grandfather to sort of accompany him during this time of sadness.

The four-poster bed where my grandma took her last breath was dismantled and taken downstairs for cleaning. My grandpa decided to roll out a mat and sleep on the area where the coffin was placed. I lay beside him with our feet towards the stairs and our heads towards the west window. We did not use any mosquito net because to do so would necessitate driving nails on the walls with a hammer, which we did not have in the house.

We were so tired that we easily succumbed to sleep.

Towards midnight, I was awakened by my tri-colored cat, which was scratching my left foot with its claws. I tried to drive it away. My grandpa was fast asleep. He was recovering for the several nights that he hardly slept. The cat played with my feet again so I wrapped them well with the blanket.

I was trying to return to fall asleep again when I heard somebody locking the front door downstairs. It must be my father, so I thought.

He must have gone out to play mahjong with his friends and just gone back now.

I waited for him to come up. Several minutes had passed and still he was not visible. He must have gone to the toilet to urinate, so I thought. After some time, I heard someone climbing the stairs. At last, he's coming up, so I thought as I anticipated his coming up. The footsteps on the stairs continued, but wait, they're too far in between. If that were my father, he would have reached the top of the stairs in no time. I started to become suspicious, who could this be? Then it dawned on my mind that it was the way my "ima" climb the stairs, forceful yet far in between because of her age.

I tried to wake my grandpa, whispering "Anda" several times at the same time shaking his left arm. He would not wake up. I called him again softly because I don't want whoever was in the stairs to know that I was awake. My grandpa could not be awakened, he was fast asleep. The cat cuddled itself by my legs and I in turn pulled the rest of the blanket over my head.

The footsteps were already on top of the stairs. The wooden floors were creaking towards my left side. I know that my "ima" had returned to take a last look at me. I nudged my grandpa repeatedly until he woke up. My lower jaw was almost trembling with fear and my whole body was shaking in fear. The creaking of the floor beside me stopped as my grandfather woke up. I told him that the ghost of my grandma was haunting me. He wanted to know where and if she said anything. I told him that I heard the footsteps coming to me but that I did not see anything because I covered my head with the blanket.

Having said that, I stood up, ran towards the master's bedroom. Trembling all over, I knocked on my parent's bedroom until they opened up. When my mother opened the door, I hurriedly went in and told them that there was a ghost in the house. I was so surprised to see my father in the room. So definitely, it was not him who just came up the stairs. I shuddered as I told them what I heard. It must be the cat, they said. But I could not be convinced because it was the cat that woke me. I never slept with my grandfather again after that incident, ever.

CAMPING AT CAMP GREZAR

When I was in first year high school aged 12, I had a recurring dream. It was about being in a rural backyard planted with some "madre de cacao" trees… at night. The feeling was usually eerie and gloomy yet I was playing with some neighborhood children… at night. I probably dreamt about that scene three times.

I was already a high school freshman at that time and though we were supposed to take up military training, in that school, Torres High School in Gagalangin, Tondo, Manila we were instead trained as Boy Scouts for the first two years and allowed to have military training only for the third and fourth year. There were those, however, who opted to continue their Boy Scout training even in their third and fourth years.

We were under the Scoutmaster by the name of Sir Rodolfo Gutierrez. One of the usual scouting activities was camping. Our first camping activity was at Camp Grezar in Novaliches, Quezon City but to get there we were required to hike from our high school location in Tondo to the camp in Novaliches which was a good eight (8) kilometers away. I was the scribe of our patrol so I had to map our route as we walk towards our destination. Being quite small at 4'11" with the taller scouts not more than 5'4" in height, our strides were small such that when we got to our destination it was almost four in the afternoon.

The entrance to the Camp was about half a kilometer away from the main road so it cannot be seen from the main road. The atmosphere at the Camp was much different from the polluted City where we came from because it had so many trees and man-made pools thus making one feel cool.

On reaching the place, we were assigned different tasks. Some set up the tents, others started preparing our food, there were those who gathered firewood and still others were sent on errands. It was already getting dark when I was tasked to go to the main road to buy some supplies from one of the stores there. Together with another scout we went towards the store. On getting back to the camp, it was already dark. We were almost at the gate of the Camp when I happened to look towards my left. I saw some "madre de cacao" trees growing on the vacant lot. I felt the same eeriness that I felt during the recurring dreams and the time was dark and gloomy. Within me, I know that it was the place that I kept seeing in my dream. Thus, began the series of dreams that eventually come true. Later on, I would learn that psychics call this kind of experience as "creative precognition."

Sometimes I would have doubts myself whether I really dreamt about a certain event before it happened so I resorted to listing down any vivid dream that I had so that I could go back to it when the actual event had happened just to be sure that I was not just imagining things.

BRIEF ENCOUNTER, LASTING FRIENDSHIP

My paternal grandparents, the Fernandezes, were a religious couple. They always pray before going to bed or recite the rosary when the occasion called for it.

In a way, I was influenced by their religiosity such that when I was in high school, I decided to join the Student Catholic Action.

The Student Catholic Action, aside from its regular catechism class, holds an annual conference in Baguio City, the summer capital of the Philippines famous for its pine trees, woodcarvings, fresh vegetables, fruit preserves, picturesque views and fresh cold air.

In December of 1965, I was invited to the conference together with five other representatives from our group. We were in third year high school then.I was so excited because that would be the first time I would experience Baguio.

The long-haul trains were still running then. The train ride will also be a first for me. Actually, the rails were located at the back of my grandma Baning's house in Manila. However, I had to go to the Tutuban train station to buy my ticket. Besides, the train will not stop at the back of our house no matter what, except for an accident.

My "Lola Baning" accompanied me to the train station. After buying my ticket to Damortis, a town in La Union where we had to disembark to transfer to a Philippine National Railways bus bound for Baguio, I waved goodbye to her and boarded the train.

There were so many students from different high schools, both public and private, in the train. I caught a glimpse of some of my schoolmates but they were seated quite far from where I was so I decided to stay put in my seat.

I stayed awake for the duration of the train ride of five hours because I wanted to see the scenery along the way. I don't remember talking neither with my seatmate nor with the two other passengers across us. I was that shy or snooty for some people.

On reaching Damortis, we got down the train and transferred to the waiting buses, also owned by the train company. They were called PNR buses. The bus ride to Baguio passes by the Kennon Road, a network of zigzag roads at the edge of deep ravines. It was an exciting ride bordering on danger as the buses course up the mountainsides. Everybody knew that one mistake of the driver will plunge the bus to the ravine down below. The drivers were used to the roads and we reached the city of pines without any untoward incident. It took approximately an hour to get to the St. Louis University where we stayed for the conference and for our lodging.

All students were billeted at the school's dormitory. This particular conference was intended for boys only so no female SCA member was around. There was this one huge hall with so many beds in the dormitory. We were told to occupy any bed that we want. I went directly to the bed nearest the huge double door serving as hall entrance.

It was announced that all meals from breakfast to dinner would be at the La Patria, a restaurant located along Session Road just below the Baguio Cathedral. St. Louis University is located at the back of the Cathedral. All conferences will be held at the St. Louis Auditorium at the back of the Cathedral.

Since it was already late in the afternoon, we were told to proceed to the university chapel for the compline (night prayers) then to the La Patria for our dinner. I still remember the first stanza of the SCA song, which goes:

> An army of youth flying the standards of truth
> We are soldiers of Christ, the Lord!

I don't remember the rest of the song; it was a long, long time ago.

On the first day of the conference, everybody woke up early at the sound of the warning bell and scampered to the common bathroom to do his early morning rituals. I was quite small then, about 4' 11" with a proportionately small body. I had a round face (moon face, as the Chinese would say) and almond eyes. I suppose I took after my great great grandfather as far as the eyes are concerned.

I could not assert myself into the long line of big boys ahead of me so on hearing someone announce that there was a water source downstairs where one could take a bath or wash his face or brush his teeth, I ran down the stairs together with some other boys.

There were still some boys bathing from the faucets with icy cold water. I wondered how they could stand the cold, it was freezing cold and I was trembling all over. I was one among the last to bather with the very cold water. I had to go through it; otherwise, I might emit a foul smell at the conference. After washing off the soap from my body, I was ready to leave for the dormitory upstairs so I can change clothes when I heard a voice pleading for me to wait for him. I turned around and I saw under the shower a handsome boy with almond eyes under the shower imploring me to wait up for him. Apparently, all the rest of the boys had rushed to the La Patria for breakfast and we were the only two boys left behind.

Hesitantly, I said yes, and then I watched as he hurriedly took a shower of icy cold water. He was trembling, too due to the cold water. His name is Alfonso Leong from Araullo High School located at the corner of Taft Avenue and United Nations Avenue in the heart of Manila.

When he was through, we raced through the stairs and went up the dormitory. It turned out that his bed was only a bed away from mine. There was somebody occupying a bed between us. By the way, the beds were all double deckers and we were both occupying the beds underneath.

We quickly dried our wet bodies with water still dripping from our hair, covered our bodies with our own towels and wore the clothes intended for that day…. In a great hurry!

We raced half running to the restaurant to eat. After taking a quick breakfast, we proceeded to the auditorium for the conference. We belonged to different cells (groups) but we can see each other from where we were.

From then on, we were always together for every meal and every free time after each day's conference.

On our second morning in Baguio, there was a commotion as we woke up in the morning. Somebody played a joke on the participants by applying toothpaste on their foreheads as they sleep. There were those who laughed while others grudgingly shouted invectives when they found out they had toothpaste on their foreheads. Then everybody started laughing on one another.

Alfonso was still asleep. I approached his bed to wake him up. I tapped his right shoulder and told him that he had toothpaste on his forehead when he opened his eyes. I meant to laugh at him as a joke. Suddenly, he pointed to my forehead and heartily laughed as he saw that I, too, had toothpaste on my forehead.

During lunch break that day, we walked along Session Road and came upon the market place. We saw a couple of local girls standing. Al approached them and introduced himself. The girls sensing that we were from Manila seemed interested in us and told him their names. After a brief conversation, Alfonso looked at his watch and noticed it was time to go back to the conference. The girls invited us to visit them that evening. They gave directions to Al on where they could be found. We hurriedly went back to St. Louis for the conference.

That evening was so cold. After dinner, Al requested for us to go to the market place again, to see the girls we met earlier during the day. We were both wearing thick sweaters and long pants and still we could feel the coldness into our bones. Al placed his arms around my shoulder as we strode down Session Road to the market. We talked as we walked until we reached the destination. The market was quite close to the university but we had a 10:00 p.m. curfew so we must hurry.

On reaching the market, Al asked for directions. We were directed to go to the second floor so we proceeded there. It turned out that it was a place for selling slaughtered meat. But some stalls were selling cooked food. That was probably the reason why the girls said their parents operate a restaurant.

Al asked for directions on where to locate the girls. We saw them in one of the stalls apparently waiting for us. However, there was another young man who was throwing sharp looks at us. He could probably be an older brother or an admirer of one of the girls. I did not go near the girls, as I was wary of the lurking danger. Most people there were holding very sharp knives by reason of their business. Besides, it was quite dark. The place lights for business very early in the morning though.

Maybe Al sensed that something could go wrong in that place. Maybe he, too, noticed the sharp look from the young man nearby. After a few minutes, he said goodbye to the girls and said, "Let's go!"

On the way back to the dormitory he told me that he never expected that the restaurant the girls were talking about was an eatery surrounded by stalls selling slaughtered animals. Besides he thought that the place could be dangerous for strangers like us.

The third day was the last day of our stay in Baguio. That meant we had to do our shopping for "pasalubong" (gifts for relatives and friends) inherent from the place during lunch and evening breaks. Al and I went back to the market but only to buy some food items and some souvenirs from the stalls fronting Session Road.

The following morning, after taking breakfast, we were directed to the PNR buses, which will bring us to the train station in Damortis.

We were facing each other on the train. Most of the time, we were looking at the window for the sceneries. We were both unusually quiet the whole train ride to Manila. No one dared tell a joke or a story. It was as if we were both savoring the last few hours of our togetherness. Whenever I see that he could be deep in thought while looking outside, I would throw a glimpse at his good-looking face with a carefully pomaded hair. We both avoided looking at each other during the trip.

When the train reached the Tutuban Station in Manila it came to a halt. We stood up and for the last time held each other's hand in farewell. It was a difficult situation for us. I knew that he, too, had a heavy heart full of sadness as we said our goodbyes.

It was as if I could sense that I would not be able to see him again; that our meeting in Baguio was just by perchance; a brief, intimate friendship that I will treasure for as long as I live. Somehow, I had the feeling that he was my brother, perhaps from a previous lifetime.

I have never seen him again personally but I got to talk to him on the phone 20 years later. I was introduced to a close female friend of his elder brother who apparently knew Al was my friend. Could it be that he was talking about our having met me to people he knew?

I called him up. I was then working with a big conglomerate and he was connected with the electronic data processing center of another big corporation. We talked briefly on the phone. I asked him if he still remembers me to which he enthusiastically said, "Yes." We talked for a while but could not carry on the conversation. I told him, I would see him one time but I never found the time. I still wanted to see him to find out what happened to his life, his family, his job and so on. And I will relate to him what happened to mine.

The Ancient Wisdom teaches about reincarnation; in which process we are born to a family or meet friends whom we come to love dearly.

Those friends who genuinely love each other very much could be identical twins in a future life if both have the same gender when born or they could be paternal twins if they have different genders when reborn.

On the other hand, mortal enemies could be Siamese twins on the extreme.

The reason why mortal enemies are joined physically by reason of birth is for them to be able to learn tolerance for each other.

In my case, could it be that Alfonso was a dear friend or a beloved brother in a **previous lifetime** but that we were not destined to be together in this?

FEAR OF THE UNSEEN

I was sixteen years old when I enrolled as a freshman at the University of the Philippines in Diliman, Quezon City. UP is the foremost State University in the country.

The year before, I was one among the many aspirants from my school, Torres High School, then the biggest secondary school in terms of enrollees, who took up the entrance examinations at the Ateneo de Loyola University along Katipunan Road in Quezon City. We were hoping to get a scholarship because those of us from the public school could not afford the high tuition fees that the private religious schools charge.

I passed the qualifying exams but did not qualify for any scholarship. Well, my father planned to enroll me at San Beda College, anyway. At that time, it was the best school for law students with a very high number of students passing the board exams. My father wanted me to be a CPA-Lawyer, which I did not particularly like because I wanted to be either an architect or a painter.

I once mentioned to him that my Aunt Pilarica Mendoza, his first cousin, suggested that I may perhaps be best suited to degree in architecture because she saw some promise in me with the drawings I did for her daughter who was studying then at the Philippine Women's University taking up Nutrition. My father immediately brushed aside my suggestion and said if I could just finish any four-year commerce course, he could pull some strings and get me a job at the Philippine National Bank even as a bank clerk. Then, he said I could continue studying law on my own income.

As fate would have it, I instead ended up enrolling at the University of the Philippines. It turned out that in order to be able to enroll in any of the well-known universities and colleges in Metro Manila, one had to take the entrance tests. These were usually given several months before the enrollment in June of each year. I did not know about those regulations nor did my parents who were living in the province, some 65 kilometers away from Manila.

I think God had been very supportive of me because the other remaining choices were University of Sto. Tomas located in Sampaloc, Manila and De La Salle College located in Malate, Manila. But after considering the tuition costs in those schools plus the fact that I was not able to take up the entrance tests in any of them, my situation appeared hopeless. Then my father remembered my baptismal godfather's brother who worked with the registrar's office at the University of the Philippines in Diliman.

That was perhaps the answer to my desire to get out of the dominion of my maternal grandmother with whom I was living for the past six years. UP was located very far from Manila and to commute would take more than an hour even without traffic. More than that it would entail a lot of transport fares. The entrance exams had been given several months back and the list of accepted students was already posted when my father talked to my godfather's brother. When he saw my report card, he said there was no need to take up the entrance exams because I ranked 10.5 out of more than a thousand students from my high school. In the case of other schools in the provinces, U.P. exempts only the Valedictorian and Salutatorian from taking the entrance exams. All the rest of the students had to take it.

Enrolling at UP was providential for me because the tuition fee was so low compared with the other private colleges and universities because it is a government school. Also, the dormitory lodgings and food prices were socialized such that for twenty-five pesos a month, one can avail of a decent bed space together with three other students in the room.

I opted to stay at the Molave Residence Hall, a dormitory for freshmen. Its counterpart dormitory for women was the Ylang-ylang Residence Hall.

Molave Residence Hall looked massive and sprawling with its two dormitory wings, the east and the west wings. I was assigned to the east wing, room 113. When I checked in, someone from Davao was already there. His name is Antonio Ng, valedictorian of Ateneo de Davao, very studious Chinese mestizo. Presently, I learned that he is the president of AMKOR-ANAM, a Filipino-Korean electronics joint venture company in the Philippines.

Another dorm mate staying at room 103 who also was my block–mate in all my first semester courses was Rafael Baylosis from Tarlac, valedictorian of his high school, too. Eventually, he would become prominent as secretary-general of the communist-leaning National Democratic Front.

I remember we had three "big brods", sophomore students who were given free lodging in the dormitory on the condition that they will look after the welfare of the freshmen staying in the dorm. One was Bob Carson, who later became a pharmaceutical salesman (that was the last I learned about him), the other one was Manny Ortega, a very handsome guy who I believe became a lawyer or something, then there was Ramoncito Abad who eventually became the president of the Philippine National Construction Corporation and later the Chairman of the Development Bank of the Philippines.

I wont describe or talk about the personalities who occupied the dormitory during that time, rather I would talk about what I have experienced one midnight at the lobby of the dormitory.

I have an exam the following day in one of the subjects that I really like, Asian Civilizations. The subject matter that the examinations will cover was quite lengthy such that my friends who I used to study with already called it a night by eleven o'clock. We used to stay at the mezzanine just over the dormitory entrance. The dorm clerks already locked the front door and decided to turn in. In short, I was the only one left at the mezzanine overlooking the main mess hall.

I was already getting tired with what I was reading but I had to finish it. Bored with the mezzanine floor, I decided to go down the spiral staircase and headed toward the hall at the ground floor of the west wing.

There were several lounge chairs along the perimeter of the hall; the rest was a vast expanse of floor. I decided to occupy one of the chairs by the window, slightly reclining on the soft upholstered chair. By and by, I was feeling sleepy and my eyelids were getting heavy. I decided to sit up straight; I can't afford to fall asleep without finishing the book.

Suddenly, I sensed something eerie, I looked at my watch, and it was almost midnight. I tried to dismiss what I sensed; it could just be my imagination creating scary thoughts. I looked around, I was alone, and no one else has entered the wide empty hall.

As I continued to read, I heard a sound, a long AAAH sound near my left ear, I turned around but no one was there. I suspected one of my friends might be scaring me away. I turned again to look in all directions but did not see anyone.

Then it started again, the long AAAH sound very close to my ear. I stood up, feeling all hair in my body standing on ends. I felt fear in my heart. How could I hear a sound distinctly without seeing anyone near me or in the entirety of the hall?

I heard the sound again! I was already terrified, so I took off towards the door of the hall, to the vast main mess hall, to the east wing corridor and to the confines of room 113.

Later I would hear stories that the Japanese used the Molave Residence Hall as a garrison during their occupation of the Philippines. I also learned that a lot of Filipinos and Americans were killed in that building. Could it be the **ghost** of one of those who died in that hall? An **earth-bound spirit** perhaps?

I was definite I heard the sound, it was the AAAH of a male person and he was making the sound as if breathing closely to my left ear.

TRAPPED IN THE PHYSICAL BODY

Military training has been an integral part of college education in the Philippines, probably as an offshoot of the First and Second World Wars.

In their first two years in college, students are required to take up ROTC training or Reserve Officers' Training Course. Different colleges and universities have different military training orientations. There are of course four kinds of military: air force, navy, marines and the police. In U.P., its military graduates become reserve marines in the eventuality of war.

Being one of the smallest, I was always at the front of the squad, and of course, of the platoon. Our military training was usually held on Saturdays. Other universities have theirs on Sunday mornings.

The U.P. Campus is so big, being patterned after the university towns of Europe or U.S. A. so we have enough parade grounds where our cadenced marching was practiced. Aside from practicing how to obey commands and how to march rhythmically, we also had lots of lectures on military tactics, and how to assemble-disassemble M1 rifles. I just don't know if that kind of rifle will still be useful by this time.

In first year, the leather combat boots that I bought was too tight for my feet because that was the closest size I could find when I finally had the money to purchase the shoes. Therefore, my toes really hurt after 30 minutes of marching using those shoes. Besides, my fatigue uniform was so thick and tight fitting to my body.

In addition to the strenuous marching and long periods we were required to stand at attention during parades plus the terrible heat of the sun during summer, my frail body gets tremendously tired on Saturdays.

We wake up early on Saturdays, do our mornings rituals, rush to the Canteen to eat breakfast and don our ROTC uniforms to be in time for the formation at the Parade Grounds by 8:00 a.m. On days that there were inspection parades, we were made to stand still at attention under the sun for almost four hours. Dismissal was at 12:00 noon wherein we who live at the dormitories would rush back to our respective dorms to take our lunch then hurry back to our rooms to remove those thick uniforms and hurting shoes.

On two occasions, an unusually frightening experience happened to me.

After taking a quick lunch, I would hurry back to my room at the Molave Residence Hall, removing my cap, loosening my belt and unbuttoning my shirt along the way as I walk towards the room. Upon reaching my room, I would hurriedly remove my boots to free my feet from imprisonment then remove my shirt and pants as well as undershirt so I can immediately change to more comfortable cotton shirt and short pants.

There were three of us students staying in the room and sometimes, I would come in ahead of the other two or they would be ahead of me in the room.

It was usual for me to lie down on my bed as soon as I could change to more comfortable clothes, to rest or to take a nap, whatever.

One time, as I opened the room with my key, I saw that Antonio Ng and Joseph Castro were already in the room telling stories. I went directly to my clothes cabinet and pulled out a clean shirt and short pants. After hanging my uniform, I jumped into bed. In a few minutes, I was almost asleep. My frail body was too tired that as I was lying flat on my back I had no desire to move at all.

As I was falling asleep, I suddenly had the desire to join the conversation of my roommates. That desire interrupted my sleep and my consciousness became very vivid again. However, when I was about to move my body to lie on my side so I can see my roommates sideways, I couldn't move any part of my body. My physical body was lying flat on the bed and I could not make it move in any way. I felt frantic enclosed within the body because it was as if the consciousness was trapped inside the body. I was feeling trapped inside like a bubble of air that could not pierce a hole in the skin or with no strength to even shake the walls of the body. I knew that I was inside the body and could not command it to move. My eyes were slightly open but I could not move my eyeballs. My lips were closed and could not utter even a word.

I began to imagine things. What if Joseph had a knife and he wanted to thrust it on my chest? I would be helpless! Completely helpless! I would not even be able to parry his thrust.

What if Tony got a pillow and smothers me with it? I couldn't even move my head sideways.

The thoughts were bothering me. My imagination was so fertile that I was beginning to think of so many negative possibilities that could happen to me.

I tried to move my hands to no avail. I felt I was a ping-pong ball that goes in any part of my body that I direct it to. With that I concentrated on moving even just my right forefinger. With my best efforts, I concentrated to my forefinger. My finger finally moved a little and with that tiny movement, I was able to animate my whole body again.

I was so relieved. I thought I could never move my body again.

It happened again on two other occasions. This loss of control of the physical body usually happens when one is so tired that the body really had to be rested so it can be energized again.

These kinds of experiences proved something to me, that I am not the body. Rather I am something that animates the body. However, without energy, the body cannot move and as" **consciousness**", even without the body, I could still be **aware.**

A Dream Of Foreigners

When I was about 27 years old working as Systems Analyst at Delta Motor Corporation, Philippine assembler of Toyota cars and trucks, I was one of those assigned to design the systems and procedures of Air Manila, Inc. The firm was a charter airline company owned by the majority owner of Delta Motor Corporation, the family of Mr. Ricardo Silverio, now a Congressman in Bulacan. At that time the Silverio Group had some 23 companies engaged in various businesses. Those of us employed by the management firm of Silcor Management Corporation get assigned to the various firms in the group depending on the need.

At Air Manila, three of us Analysts worked at the conference room with a very huge round table surrounded by around 20 upholstered swivel chairs. With me were Thelma Sumabat and Manolito Vicente. Thelma was a psychologist; Titus was a mechanical engineer while I was a Certified Public Accountant. During lunch break, we usually put out all the ceiling lights in the conference room after taking our lunch at the canteen nearby so that we can take a short nap by resting our bodies by bending down and resting our heads on one of our bent arms on the table while remaining seated.

On one such situation, I woke up startled. Upon checking my watch, I saw it was already 10 minutes past 1:00 p.m. so I immediately got up and went out of the room to take a leak. Titus and Thelma were still napping.

I was out for only about four minutes and got back right away. I opened the door and proceeded straight away to my chair without looking around. I was so surprised because as I raised my head after taking a seat, there was the scene that I dreamt a couple of weeks before.

There were about four Americans, big men seated opposite me, on chairs around the conference table. In a few seconds, the door swung open and in came Mr. Ricardo Silverio, president of Air Manila who occupied one of the seats across my chair. It turned out he had a meeting with the foreigners but we were not informed about it before hand. The three of us sat there dumbfounded by the turn of events.

The event was exactly as I had seen it in my dream a couple of weeks before, another case of **creative precognition.**

Attraction To Structures

When our work at Air Manila was finished, we were instructed to go back to our headquarters along Pasong Tamo Extension, which place was a far cry from the hustle and bustle of the Ayala financial district in Makati.

I was staying then at the Pope Piux XII Catholic Center Men's Dormitory. In reporting for work, I usually take the CI Lines bus because that was the only transport that went as far as Pasong Tamo. The other alternative was for me to take several jeepney rides in order to get to my destination. Taking a taxi was out of the question because we were still receiving a very small salary at that time, hardly enough to keep us surviving.

I had to go to San Marcelino Street by walking two blocks of the stretch of the United Nations Avenue so I can take the bus ride to office. The CI lines bus usually cruise San Marcelino Street and turns a little to the right upon crossing Quirino Avenue so it can continue along Leon Guinto Street up to Vito Cruz Street where it turns left and then makes a right turn towards Zobel Roxas. On reaching that street the buss makes another left turn until it crosses the South Super Highway. Then it cruises Malugay Street and turns right to Pasong Tamo, crosses Buendia and EDSA until it reaches Pasong Tamo Extension. The same route is traversed by the bus in going back to Quiapo except that since Vito Cruz is a one way street, it takes Estrada Street before turning right to Leon Guinto Street towards Manila.

I did not know for what reason my attention was always drawn to an old wooden house just beside the ice cream house situated at the corner of Estrada and Leon Guinto streets. Each time the bus passes that house, I could not help myself but take a long look at that old house even for a few seconds. That went on for several months, that extraordinary attraction. There was nothing spectacular about the house; it was an old and ordinary- looking liberation-type house, yet I felt an unexplained strong attraction to it.

When I decided to pursue my graduate studies, I enrolled at the De La Salle University Graduate School of Business. As an institute of learning it has a very good reputation and at that time had the distinction of being one of the two graduate schools in the Philippines recognized worldwide, the other one being the University of the Philippines.

De La Salle University is located along Taft Avenue near Vito Cruz Street. Estrada St. leads directly to the façade of La Salle. Therefore, Estrada ends at Taft Avenue. Leon Guinto Street, along which the old house stood is parallel to Taft Avenue and culminates at Vito Cruz Street.

I intended to take the evening classes because I had work while studying. In order to avoid travelling a long distance at night just to get home to Sta. Mesa, I decided to look for a boarding house near La Salle. The most likely place to find a boarding house was along Leon Guinto Street because it was only a block away from La Salle.

Finding no vacancy along Estrada or Leon Guinto streets, I proceeded to Vito Cruz where I found a "Wanted Boarders" sign at Aling Conching's Restaurant. I talked to the owner, a very religious woman who always attend mass yet at the same time abusive of her waitresses and house helpers. She directed her daughter, Baby, to show me the room. The daughter asked me to follow where she would go. We went out of the restaurant and turned left to Leon Guinto then crossed Estrada Street. I was taken aback when she pushed open the gate of the old wooden house that always attracted my attention.

It turned out that the house had been empty for quite awhile but that the owner leased it over to Aling Conching just recently. She's turning the ground floor into a restaurant and the second floor into a boarding house. As it turned out, I was only one of the three boarders who would stay at the second floor during regular semesters. During summer, there was a group of teachers who would stay for about two months for summer classes.

I had a roommate in the room, a second year college student by the name of Cesar Montaniel who was also studying at La Salle taking up engineering. It turned out his elder brother, Jun Montaniel was my office mate at SGV & Company, which was my first job.

The restaurant downstairs was not so successful and the rooms upstairs had not been filled up with boarders so after a year, Aling Conching closed the facility and transferred us to the second floor of a house at the corner of Vito Cruz and Leon Guinto, fronting the St. Scholastica Chapel. At the ground floor of the house was a drug store. It was very near Aling Conching's original restaurant where we usually took our meals.

Today, the house that intrigued me was no longer there. I recently passed by the street and what I saw was a multi story building that was built in its stead.

Another structure attracted me extraordinarily sometime in 1975. It was located along Paseo de Roxas St., a block away from Ayala Avenue. It was a four-story building owned and being used by the Insular Bank of Asia and America.

I already had a vehicle at that time, a Toyota Corolla that I use in going around Makati and to the provinces. I don't know why but whenever I pass that building I wanted to go in and see how it looked inside. Whenever I pass by Paseo de Roxas, I can't help but take a long look at that building.

The following year, 1976, I met a person by the name of Antonio Manalo. It turned out that he was working for the Head Office Branch of Insular Bank of Asia and America as one of the accounting staff.

Since then, I used to frequent the mezzanine of the building where the accounting staffs of IBAA were holding office.

In this case, it was probably the person who I was destined to meet that drew my attention to the building.

Can it be true then, that we can somehow feel our **predestiny**?

MIND POWER SEMINAR

A deal was made between our company Delta Motor Corporation, and self-styled guru Rolando Carbonell, famous for the poem he wrote entitled "Beyond Forgetting". Mr. Carbonell will conduct his Mind Power seminars for our 20 or so top executives in exchange for a brand new Toyota Crown model 1975.

Quite embarrassed, I approached Thelma Sumabat a colleague at the Systems Group who was close to the vice-president for administrative services. I was intrigued with the subject matters to be taken up such as telepathy, psychokinesis, dream interpretation, regression, levitation and meditation that I requested her to see if I can be accommodated in the seminar.

I learned that some staff of Marketing Department had been accommodated into the seminar though they were not managers upon the intercession of their boss, Mr. Luis Feliciano, Vice-President for Marketing, They were Zonnie Velasco, Erlinda Pena and Ludina Garcia.

Carbonell was then married to Letty Liboon, formerly a starlet. The latter would assist in the sessions that we attended. At the sessions, we would come to meet such notable personalities as Tita Munoz, an actress of yesteryears and Zita Zabarte, a rich socialite. There were some other participants whose names I have already forgotten.

Sessions were held at the Ermita Center located along Roxas Boulevard by the Manila Bay. To demonstrate telepathy and to find out who among us has that talent, we were divided into two groups and paired off. One group remained at the eight floor of the building while the second group was asked to go down to the second floor. At a given signal, the members of the first group ware instructed to each think of

57

an object of his choice for about ten to fifteen minutes. At the same time the members of the other group were instructed to keep their minds open and try to perceive what his partner was thinking of. Then the process was repeated with the second group doing the thinking this time. Then all participants were gathered together and asked to report what each one had perceived. While I would say that only 20% correctly perceived the message sent to them by their partner and the rest either perceived incorrectly or missed, the exercise just showed that there really was such a thing as telepathy.

Other topics discussed and demonstrated that I still remember were dream interpretation, regression and "life readings" done by a couple of very young psychics. Some of the past lives I lived, according to the young reader were as a Spanish dancer (female), a Japanese Emperor, a Mongolian prince, a craftsman, an Egyptian princess and other incarnations.

What turned out to be the most memorable part of the sessions was the guided meditations where we were required to sit (at least try) in lotus posture in the darkened hall while Mr. Carbonell guided our visualizations. After about 30 minutes of guided meditations, Mr. Carbonell was guiding our consciousness back to the room when we heard somebody crying. When I looked back, it was Linda Pena, an office mate and a very close friend. The reason she was crying was due to the fact that while the guided meditations had been finished, she has lost control of her physical body. Her upper arms remained floating in the air and she could not will them to drop by her sides. Everybody was amazed while Mr. Carbonell tried his best to get the attention of Linda and to command her to return to normal. It took several attempts before Linda got control of herself again.

I would say that the Mind Power sessions was my first formal introduction to the **esoteric world** and the **world of psychism**. It was also instrumental in a way for my going to the **Divine Wisdom School**.

Had Linda not lost control of her physical body, she would not have been invited to the Divine Wisdom School. In turn, I would not have gone to that school were it not for the encouragement of Linda.

GRANDPA'S LOVE

Almost a decade after grandma's death, my grandfather succumbed to age old illness. However, I suspect he must have had high blood pressure because once in a while he stumbles when he gets dizzy. He was 92 when he died as estimated by my father. That generation of folks did not know their exact dates of birth so that their ages were but estimates. Their parents did not bother to list down their dates of birth since most of them had not had any education at all.

I had just started working for a reputable accounting firm along Ayala Street in Makati yet I usually go home to Bulacan on weekends to have my dirty clothes laundered and to pick up my freshly washed and ironed clothes which my mother coordinates with a local laundry woman.

My sisters told me that after coming from the cockpit, my grandfather had a terrible fall. His eldest son, on hearing about the accident decided to pick up "anda" and bring him to his home since he knew that no one could attend to my grandpa because both my parents had to go to work and my sisters were all going to school. After a few days, grandpa insisted on returning back to our house. I knew that the attitude of both my parents toward him hurts him emotionally but I continue to be his favorite grandson because whenever he falls and I was around, I was quick to respond to him in spite of my frail body.

He would always buy me fresh pineapple, fresh sugar cane beet or other sugary delicacies whenever he sensed that I was around. He would even attempt to go as close to my face just so he could see my features in spite of his defective eyesight. One time, my sister Lerrie told me that "anda" had gone senile and doesn't recognize even his own children. I went to his room to see how he was doing. He opened his eyes upon hearing my voice and asked how I was. He was so ill and yet it was my health that he was worried about. I tried my best to control the tears welling in my eyes.

The day after I left for Manila to report for work, my father came again to fetch me. My grandfather had died. This time the remains were displayed at the ground floor of our house. Many relatives came. It was an occasion for a re-union among family members. This time I did not have that feeling of excitement that I felt when my grandmother died.

My grandfather's love for me was made manifest eight years later. I was already working with Delta Motor Corporation, assembler and distributor of Toyota cars, trucks and forklifts and one of the more progressive firms in the Philippines at that time.

I dreamt that I was taking an afternoon nap in the bedroom at the second floor of the house. In the dream I saw that all outer walls of the second floor were torn down and only some partitions in the middle of the house remained. Moreover, though it was daytime, the surrounding was hazy and there was no heat from the afternoon sun. I was taking a nap in the dream when I felt something stir from the base of the stairs at the ground floor. I tried to peep through a hole on the floor, I saw it was my dead grandfather who was starting to climb the stairs. Fear gripped me; I could hear my heart beat faster, so I tried to look for a place to hide. The walls were low so I could only crouch and move about slowly. Grandpa was already on the second floor but I could not hear any creaking of the floor. I tried to look at him while he was facing on the other direction looking for me. He was wearing clean white clothes but he did not have any feet, he was floating on air. He looked much younger, too, than when he died.

He knew I was hiding from him. He also knew that I could see him. Though there were some obstructions between us, he was only a couple of feet away from me. Looking at my direction, he lovingly communicated to me, without opening his mouth, a message that I perceived, "I know you are not happy with your work now!"

That was the only message he imparted but it affected me so much. I knew he was so sincere in looking after my welfare that even though he was no longer here on the physical plane, he was still concerned after my welfare. It was probably eight o'clock when I woke up that morning and I woke up crying. I cried to my heart's content because I was deeply touched by that gesture of my grandfather. When he was still alive, I was constrained to show my concern for him because my parents had a conflict with him. I don't know if my father will admit this now or if he will still remember that.

After several months, I resigned from my work as Assistant Treasurer of Delta Motor Corporation. My grandfather was right, I was no longer happy with my work and he told me his message **telepathically.**

Astral Travel

Ka Nitoy, a spiritual teacher used to say that "You are not the body, you are something else using the physical body as a vehicle for expression on the physical plane."

"The 'I' is the ego and yet you are not the ego," he would continue.

What are we then so-called human beings?

To use me as an example, according to Ka Nitoy, I am the personality called Hector Fernandez and what comprises the personality are the physical body (and all its organs), the emotional body and the mental body. These bodies are all enclosed in an ovoid called the causal body. The totality of all these interpenetrating bodies which is ovoid in shape is called the "aura".

In addition there is what is called an etheric body. This body may still be considered as a gross body but not visible to the naked eye unless one is a clairvoyant. It is slightly bigger than the physical body but follows its contours. It is vital because through it energy from the sun passes to animate the physical body. Without the energized etheric double we cannot physically move or else we would seem "lifeless".

"Why don't you prove to yourselves that you are not the body? I will teach you the technique," Ka Nitoy would challenge us.

One time, as we were talking with him as a small informal group, we asked him how to do astral travelling.

He did not hesitate to tell us how to do it but with caution. He warned us that the astral world is so fluidic that any thought of anyone could create forms, thought forms. These could be beautiful or grotesque depending on the thoughts of the entities there.

One night, I decided to try getting out of my physical body consciously at will. I switched on the electric fan to medium speed facing the direction of my bed because there were quite a number of mosquitoes in the room then put off the light.

I lay still and straight but comfortably on my bed, head propped up by a pillow. Then I covered my legs up to my waist with a blanket. Finally, I raised both my arms from the elbow then told myself that I was going to fall asleep. My eyes were half closed such that I was at the threshold of being awake and being asleep.

In time my eyelids got real heavy and every time I would fall asleep my arms would fall down from their vertical position. Each time my arms fell, I would be startled and be awakened. It happened several times until at about 12:30 a.m. I fell asleep without losing consciousness. I was able to keep my arms upright though my eyes were closed and I was falling into slumber.

The surrounding was so dark and yet I know precisely where my body was. I know my body was in the room lying horizontally on the bed. Little by little, I felt my consciousness rise inch by inch from my physical body. When it was out halfway towards the top of the head I remembered the warning that Ka Nitoy gave us regarding the astral plane. It caused fear in me and suddenly, I sensed that my consciousness slid back into the body.

I remember Ka Nitoy saying that fear serves as a brake for a person travelling in the etheric or astral planes. We have the so-called "silver cord" attached to the heart with one end attached to the soul. When one has an out of body experience and felt fear in any way, the silver cord will contract and pull him back to his body.

According to him, if that "silver cord" will snap as it sometimes do, the soul will no longer be able to go back to the physical body and the person will die. In the Philippines, such deaths were considered as due to "bangungot" or as a consequence of a horrible dream.

That experiment, though not fully successful proved to me that I am not this physical body but rather the soul or **consciousness** that uses the different bodies in order to be able to express in the physical realm.

LOVE AT FIRST GLANCE

My "confirmation" godfather, Iñigo S. Andres and his wife Dra. Filomena Radoc-Andres had an adopted son. They married late and were unable to produce any children so they adopted a child and named him Edgar.

Nana Mena doted on the adopted child very much and worked hard to be able to send him to the best schools and to give him the best comforts in life.

Edgar did not have any idea that he was adopted. He learned about it only when he got married. Actually, the family migrated to Hawaii first where Tito Edgar worked first as a busboy in a hotel before getting a job in the mainland U.S.A. I call him Tito (Uncle) because although I am much older than him since his foster father is my maternal grandmother's brother). In short, after several years of stay in Hawaii, the family decided to relocate to the mainland, to Long Beach, California in particular.

I was there in their Sta. Mesa, Manila house when the family first left for the State of Hawaii. I had to be around because they requested me and my sisters to stay and look after their house while they were away.

After almost a year, the couple went back to Manila for a short vacation. When they came back, I and my sisters Girlie and Lerrie transferred residence to Bangkal, Makati with the help of an Italian priest, Rev. Father Pierangelo Quaranta who arranged for our accommodations.

The Andres couple went back to the mainland United States after their vacation and rented an apartment in Long Beach. Nana Mena worked in a hospital while Tata Onying worked as gardener for the City of Long Beach. Tito Edgar was accepted in the U.S. Navy's computer department in San Diego. Lola Nitay and some of her nieces from Angat, Bulacan were tapped to look after their house in Manila.

I heard from the Andres family again after almost two years. The family will be coming for a vacation and to make preparations for an elaborate wedding for Tito Edgar and Josie Gonzales, his sweetheart of several years.

I was introduced briefly to Josie on the wedding day at the hotel reception. The wedding was held at the Greenhills Church in San Juan but because there were so many important people who came. Being a nobody, I just kept to the sidelines.

I met Josie again when Tito Edgar and his parents left for the United States a few days after the wedding. She had to wait a few months before she can follow to the USA so she opted to continue working in the meantime. From Makati, I drove to Sta. Mesa to bid goodbye to the family. It was there where I met Josie again. I was re-introduced to her and we talked briefly about our jobs. It turned out that our offices in Makati were just two buildings apart. With her was her best friend Olive. Josie invited me to visit her office.

I called her up a couple of days later to find out where I could find her. I went over to her office. She mentioned to me that her friends in the office would go to the disco. She asked if I could come so she could pair me off with her best friend who was nursing a broken heart. She wanted to know if I would be interested in dating Olive Valencia.

When I first saw Olive she was haggard looking, so thin and so tan but when I met her again at the disco, she was starting to perk up a bit.

I was then working with the assembler of Toyota while Olive was working as secretary at the plant of Mitsubishi Motors in Cainta. After that I would be seeing Olive at her family's Pasig residence on Sunday afternoons or call her up on the phone to find out how she was doing. However, the lines were so bad that I had to speak on top of my voice so she could hear me. Still we found it difficult to understand one another.

Several weeks later she was looking healthy and very fair complexioned. It turned out she has some Spanish blood. Sometimes she would mention to me that she will go to Baclaran Church to attend mass, which is very far from her place of work but quite near mine. I would ask her which side of the church she would stay and meet her there.

Whenever there were parties at the house of Josie's sister in Greenhills where she used to stay with her mother, she would invite me so I could meet Olive there.

Olive's father was all right but I could not stand her mother who was always shouting on top of her voice and cursing her children even when there were visitors in their house. I just don't know if it was her way of letting the visitors know that they were not welcome. I knew that Olive resented her mother's ways very much except that she could not control her. You could see the embarrassment on her face whenever her mother starts her litany of curses.

One time, I was calling Olive at her office but could not understand what she was saying. I did understand that she had to stay late at night because of overtime work. I told her I would come over and see her. I was starting to fall in love with her and in a time of inspiration was able to compose a poem entitled " The Chocolate Nymph" (Olive was very fond of chocolates). I went to her office and sheepishly handed her a bar of chocolate with the poem. I could see that she was really busy but still took time out to see me at the lobby. She urged me to leave instead of wait for her because she was not sure what time she would be able to finish her work. I insisted on waiting.

It was almost midnight when she finished her work. I brought her to her parent's house where she was staying. We were talking along the way, mostly about Josie and her husband. It turned out Josie learned about Tito Edgar's being an adopted child from a friend who was a neighbor of the Andres family.

Actually, Josie confronted me about that issue already and I had no recourse but say, "He may be adopted but Nana Mena and Tata Onying loved him more than a son!" Eventually, Josie will tell Tito Edgar about his being and adopted child and thus cause a big rift in the family.

Well, after that night that I brought Olive to her place, I got so busy with office work. I had to work everyday till ten in the evening because we had to prepare discussion materials for the review of the performance of the subsidiary companies of Silcor Management Corporation, mother firm of Delta Motor Corporation.

I decided to call up Olive one night at around nine thirty in the evening. The line was so bad that I really had to shout on the phone. I could hear her voice on the other line but she must be having a tantrum and after saying something, which I could not distinctly understand, she banged the phone. I was shocked by that display of arrogance and did not call her again, ever.

In the meanwhile, my friend Ernie Forteza called up to ask me if I wanted to attend a study session about Theosophy in one of the Lodges. I went to his place in Pasay City to fetch him. I parked the car along Aurora Street near the corner of Juan Luna Street then walked the distance towards his home. I called out his name as I got near the gate of their house. Their house is erected some ten meters away from the gate and there was a one meter wide cemented walkway leading to their door. His aunties' house was only a meter away from the gate and a worn out screened door was attached to the doorjamb.

"He is inside the house changing clothes," I heard a sweet voice say. I looked up towards my left. There was a two-step stair leading to the door of the house of Ernie's aunties.

There was a bright fluorescent light inside the house and its strong light was blocked by the figure of a young woman dressed in tattered duster dress. The television was on and apparently; the woman was watching the show from the door.

She smiled shyly to me while gathering her clothes towards her body to try to conceal the torn portions. What I found ironic was that I was instantly mesmerized by the voice and smile of that lady standing against the light in her old torn duster. Hers was the sweetest smile I've seen in my entire life.

She must have noticed my bewilderment because I used to frequent the place but I have never seen her. So she volunteered that she is a younger sister of my friend Ernie. She seemed familiar as to who I was. I asked her what she does and I was told that she worked in a Makati firm doing payroll work. Then Ernie went out the house and I bid farewell to Milen.

I could not explain my feelings that night. I was so happy to have met Milen.

Two days later, I could no longer contain myself so I looked for the telephone number of the firm she mentioned to me and tried to give her a call. She was so cordial on the phone and I offered to pick her up after office hours. At that time they held offices along EDSA Avenue near Guadalupe Bridge.

By five p.m. I hurriedly went to my car and drove to her place of office. I parked in front of the building and asked the guard if Milen was still inside the building. The guard called her and she hastily went out. I opened the car door for her and then drove to Makati Business district. I invited her for an ice cream in Quad then while eating asked her if she might want to see a movie. She hesitated for a moment, glanced at her watch and said, "Yes".

In the movie house, I held her hand and she did not object. That was the beginning of our instant love relationship.

Immediately before that, I used to visit Olive on Sunday afternoons. I usually ask a close friend to tag along so I won't feel awkward or run out of topics to discuss. In short I was courting Olive. Most of the time I would ask Tony Manalo who lives in Pasig to go with me. Sometimes, I would ask Ernie to accompany me. Tony and Olive jibed along well.

However, in the case of Ernie, I would learn later that he did not feel comfortable with Olive. On the other hand, Olive told me also that she liked Tony better than Ernie.

After that movie date with Milen I noticed I was trying to distance myself from Olive. There was an affair at the Westin Philippine Plaza Hotel one time for which I was given two free tickets. I could bring along someone as a date but I thought Olive's place was quite far from my office in Makati to fetch her. To do so means a long travel time and by the time we get to the hotel venue, the show might have been finished already. I wanted to invite Milen but she told me she had to work overtime. I did go to the function, which was a fashion show. Yet while the models were walking on the ramp, my attention was on the ceiling of the ballroom. I don't know how but what I could see was the giant image of Milen projected by my vision to the ceiling. It was a very vivid image of hers.

During the intermission, I called up Olive to say that I was at the hotel and wanted to invite her but it was quite late to do so. She said that I should not have gone to the show if I did not want to. I noticed some sadness in her voice as she was speaking so I cut the conversation short. What was bewildering to me was the intermittent flashing of Milen's face before me; in whatever direction I look, even as I was speaking with Olive.

After that incident where Olive slammed the telephone while I was talking with her, I never called up nor visited her anymore. I was courting her, true, but I never asked for a confirmation from her whether she would like to be my girlfriend. The real reason why I stopped courting her was Milen. I fell in love with Milen the instant I saw her and I believe she felt the same way, too.

I told Milen about Olive and in turn she told me that she presently had a Japanese boyfriend. Not long after, she told me that she stopped seeing her Japanese boyfriend and I told her I did the same thing with Olive.

I will not elaborate anymore what subsequently happened to our love relationship except that Olive was forced by her mother to get married to a Filipino who worked with the U.S. Navy. Olive detested the guy so much because of his ugliness (I did not get to see the guy).

Truth is Olive kept calling my office a day before the wedding and would not stop till I promised to meet with her somewhere in Makati. I mentioned a place where we could meet but on reaching the appointed place, I left my car where she could not see it. I just walked towards her Minicar. She wanted that we talk in my car but I said her car will do. She then told me that her mother agreed with the persistent suitor to marry her off and the wedding was scheduled the following day. That was her biggest problem because she did not like the guy a bit.

I'm sure if I asked her to elope with me, she would have readily agreed. But I was so in love with Milen that I told her if she really did not want to marry the guy then it was up to her. Her mother could not do anything if she did not want to. Well, the wedding pushed through and the guy brought her to California with him after a few months.

I would see her again when Josie's mother died and I came for the prayers after the funeral. I saw Olive there and waved to her from afar. I did not dare go near her. She looked at me and even though she did not say anything, her eyes told me that "If not for you, I would not have been in this situation!" I could not forget that look in her eyes, which I felt pierced my heart. I would learn later that after living with the guy for about a year, she filed for divorce and re-married to another better-looking Filipino in San Francisco.

Milen was petitioned by her parents to immigrate to the United States. When she left, I went with the rest of her sisters and aunties to the airport. The two of us had a brief chance to be alone at the airport lounge. One of their uncles, a General Forteza was managing the airport at that time so we were able to stay at the VIP Lounge. I felt so sad with her impending departure. Looking at me, Milen said, "May I see a smile?" to which I dryly smiled. I knew that had I asked her, Milen would stay but if I did I had to marry her.

What I had in mind was to allow her to experience life in the United States and when she comes back to the Philippines, then would I marry her. I just did not want her to regret not having experienced living in the United States.

During the first three months of her stay in San Jose, near San Francisco, one of her sisters who was left behind told me that Milen used to cry so much at night because she missed me a lot. I also felt the same except that I was busy with my handicraft business. Besides at that age I was no longer as emotionally attached because I've gotten used to being away from my loved ones when I was ten years old.

She would call me on the phone from time to time and say, "Hec, I love you!" To which I would say "I know, I know! or, "Same here!"

After a few months she stopped calling and writing me letters and sending huge occasion cards. Only much later did I found out that she married her American boss, a much older man. Even much older than I was.

It was our agreement that even if we don't get to marry one another, we would remain as friends, not enemies, and yet she avoids crossing my path up to now.

When I first saw Milen in her tattered clothes, I felt something in my heart. Did it mean we were **soul mates**?

When I saw Milen's giant image at the hotel ballroom, was it a creation of my **imagination**? Did I **visualize** it or was it projected by something else?

CHOCOLATE HILLS

And how could I ever forget that dream that I was observing the Chocolate hills of Bohol from a high perch? Nor that old wooden house with a garden of daisies in front?

In a few days it would be Christmas when I came across Suzette Palma, a close friend. Suzette was a widow with four children, two boys and two girls. She came to me and casually asked how I would like to go with her clan to Bohol, her place of birth. I had not been to Bohol and was not looking forward to anything exciting for the holidays so I said yes.

It will be very expensive to take the plane and besides there will be no seats available by that time so we had to take the ship together with the rest of her clan. By clan I meant her children, her sisters, brothers, nieces and nephews who were all bound for Bohol for the fiftieth wedding anniversary of her parents. Her parents now reside in Davao but they both came from Bohol. Other members of the clan were actually coming from Davao City, a very big city in terms of size located at the southernmost island of the Philippines.

Suzette and I met at a designated place then we proceeded by taxi to the local port to board the ship. On reaching the port, we found out the advance party she sent was not able to buy a ticket for me because they did not know I was coming. The ship was full of people, I suspect it was overloaded as most ships were before the holidays. The ship would be leaving in a few minutes and the crew got strict in allowing people to board the ship if they will not take the trip. At that point they did not want to let anyone without a ticket to board the ship. We were still on the dock and could not come close to the planks because there were so many people trying to board the ship.

Suzette called out in Cebuano (another local dialect) to a nephew on the upper deck. I saw her trying to catch a rolled pair of socks thrown down from the upper deck. She opened the socks discreetly and pulled out a couple of tickets. She gave one to me and held the other one. She motioned for me to follow her towards the ship. I was quite worried because the name on the ticket was not mine but we had to hurry, otherwise the ship will leave us.

We approached the planks and hastily showed the tickets to the guard as we pass him. We were allowed on board.

We hurriedly went up the upper deck and joined her relatives. The other passengers must be wondering why we were laughing heartily. They did not know that we could have been left behind had Suzette not asked for the tickets to be thrown out from the upper deck wrapped in the socks. In a few minutes the ship started to sail. We were observing the people down below. Some were still running trying to catch the ship clutching their ticket with one hand and the other grabbing a bag or two. They were left behind.

The ship docked in Cebu after almost a day of sailing. We went down and walked towards another much smaller ship bound for Bohol. The boat was small, rickety and cramped with so many people below the deck. Most passengers were instructed to go below the deck. The sea was calm and in about 45 minutes we reached our destination.

At the Bohol port, we stopped for a while to take our lunch. After that, Suzette went ahead to the cluster of jeepneys and contracted one of them.

We boarded the jeepney with our bags and proceeded to Dagohoy town but the driver was instructed to pass by the Chocolate Hills for my benefit.

The Chocolate Hills is a very famous tourist spot in Bohol. They are called chocolate hills because they look very much like the chocolate kisses in shape. The hills are small mounds of earth like oversized women's breasts neatly arranged in rows. According to reports, what makes the hills amazing other than their almost uniform size and neat arrangement was the fact that seashells can be found embed in the mounds.

Suzette called out for me to join her at the observation deck. I followed and once on the top floor, gazed at the rows of hills that I used to see only in pictures. As I trained my vision on the top of the hills, I remembered the dream I had several weeks ago. It was the exact height, the same vantage point as I had seen in my dream.

After a few minutes, we proceeded to our final destination. It was already quite late in the afternoon so we had to hurry in order to reach the place before dark. It was twilight when we did reach the house of Suzette's aunt. It was an old wooden house with garden of daisies in front, exactly as I've seen in my dream. I told Suzette about the dream I had. She just said,"Really?" and glanced at me with understanding. Suzette is a psychologist and these things are not new to her.

SUDDENLY STOP

The Babaels had their renewal of marriage vows on the 28th of December on the occasion of their golden wedding anniversary as a married couple at the Bohol Cathedral where they were previously married. Their children, grandchildren and in some instances, some great grandchildren were there to witness the occasion. Some close friends living in Bohol Island were also at the church.

After the wedding ceremony, the relatives and visitors all trooped to a restaurant for lunch In the afternoon most members of the entourage proceeded to Dagohoy town, (to the house of Suzette's aunt) where all of us from Manila stayed. Suzette's auntie was a retired schoolteacher and an old maid.

On New Year's Day, there was a lucheon party and quite a number of guests were invited to partake of the food. A long table was set up where guests were invited to sit. We sat at the far end of the table and were introduced to some people. We started to discuss about life and the hidden meanings of certain Bible passages. A few guests got so interested in the topic that even long after we had finished our meal, we just transferred to another smaller round table and continued the conversations.

One of the persons we were talking with was not from the place but was just assigned by his company to man the transmitter station of the Philippine Long Distance Telephone Company at the top of the highest mountain in the island. Before he left that day, he invited us to come and visit his office at the top of the mountain to get a good view of the whole island.

We decided to heed his invitation so the following day we took a jeepney ride up to the foot of the mountain and at a certain point set on foot because it would be too difficult for a two-wheel drive vehicle to go up the slopes of the mountain.

As I mentioned earlier, we went to Bohol via Cebu by an inter-island ship. The trip until Cebu took 21 hours. I brought along with me a couple of books to read, one of which was "The Book of Secrets" by Bhagwan Shree Rajneesh. One of the chapters that interested me was entitled "Suddenly Stop". I was reading the book on the ship and it described how the Hindus of India would swirl and dance endlessly until they get so tired at which point they would suddenly stop. He did not say what would happen if they do that so I was so curious.

On the way up the peak of the mountain, I know I would be panting and gasping for breath even before I get to the top unless I take regular rests along the way. I was asthmatic as a child and therefore gets tired easily especially when running or walking briskly. This is precisely one major reason why I am not inclined to athletic activities.

When we have scaled about three-fourths the height of the mountain, I decided to try Bhagwan's "suddenly stop" but instead of dancing I decided to tire myself by walking briskly towards the top of the mountain and the moment I feel very, very tired, I will stop suddenly.

One of Suzette's nephews was already way ahead of us while Suzette was slightly behind me. Trailing her was a niece who was a little on the plump side.

I told Suzette I would walk faster to counteract the pull of gravity which seem to be getting stronger as we go up the mountain. I walked as fast as I could up the mountain trail. After awhile I was already panting but I did not stop but rather egged on. Up ahead, I saw some trees beyond which was a steep drop. When I was near the trees I suddenly stopped.

It was daytime but the sun was hidden behind the clouds so the atmosphere was quite hazy. When I suddenly stopped, I expected that I would feel dizzy as I used to experience when as a child I get tired running while playing softball. This time it was different, I saw that my surrounding was dark and the silhouettes of the images of the trees and grasses were double. It seemed to me that it was a prelude to another realm. It was as if the other realm was superimposed to the physical reality that I know.

I got afraid because I could not see clearly where I was standing and I knew that a few feet away was the precipice. I tried to get away from the trees at the side of the trail and knelt down so I could stabilize myself. I wanted to experience the other realm but I was afraid.

The experience was unlike feeling dizzy. It was completely different from getting dizzy where all surroundings seem to be spinning and you lose your balance.

I experienced something, which I cannot describe and it could be a prelude to the experience of the **etheric plane.**

MENTAL TELEPATHY

Most people are familiar with the phrase but what is it really all about?

In late 1984, I established a firm called Amaranth Design Showcase, a trader in furniture and home décor. The Philippine economy at that time was so bad but I had no other alternative because I could not find any job. I had to make do with a few savings and to use my contacts with suppliers and friends with businesses so I could have stock to sell in the space I rented for a store.

Benigno Aquino had been assassinated in August 21, 1983 and the turmoil it created worsened the downtrend of the economy. Unemployment had turned to worse; people were trying to land jobs abroad and those who were forced to stay hardly had any money to spend. Priority spending was for food and perhaps some clothes. All other intended disbursements had to be deferred. As a result I decided I should try the export market and I should target the upper classes of society, those who have the money to buy whatever they want to buy. In this way, I don't have to mass-produce the furniture and decorative accessories I wanted to sell.

It was in this kind of export business that I met Julie Palicte of the Philippine International Trading Corporation. She was one of the Merchandisers of PITC.

As a Merchandiser, she usually accompanies foreign buyers in visiting manufacturers and suppliers of Philippine products when they visit the Philippines, most especially when there is a trade show at the Philippine International Convention Center, Philippine Trade Training Center and Philippine Trade Exhibits.

The merchandisers, like Julie would usually visit our booth at the trade show, introduce their principal (the foreign buyer) and request for calling cards, one for the buyer and one for her. The buyer would look around, inspect the products and if interested would request to see more items at the office or factory of the Philippine exporter. Later product shots or catalogs with complete description, prices and other relevant information shall be requested.

Julie had already accompanied several buyers to my booth during trade shows and to my office after the shows. She comes to the office either to accompany the buyer to see more items and transact business with me or to follow-up catalogs, photos, price lists and samples.

Julie would usually call before coming over. I did not have regular staff when I was starting my export business. I only contract for additional hands whenever there were shipments. Hence, I was the one who usually place and answer phone calls.

On several occasions, I tried to contact Julie to follow the order of her buyer or to tell her that her requests for photos were ready. In those several occasions, her local phone number would be busy. When I place the phone down, it would ring and it would be Julie. I would tell her that I was trying to call her and she would tell me that she was dialing my number.

Then there was Amy Gonzales. She was formerly my student at the Philippine School of Interior Design where I taught Basic Accounting. She was already an Architect then when she enrolled at the interior design school. I did not remember her very well but after a couple of years, we met again at the trade show I was participating in, and she talked to me about my products. After several inter-actions, she told me that she was my former student who dropped the course after a couple of weeks because she found my subject boring.

Amy became a close friend after that and from time to time, we have had collaborative interior design projects or product pictorial projects together.

I would say that we were **mentally attuned**. Whenever I thought of her, in a matter of day or two, she would be calling me up and vice-versa.

I used to have a friend in college from the University of the Philippines, a fellow member of the U.P. Student Catholic Action whom I met again two decades after I graduated from college. As we were talking about occultism, psychic abilities and the like, he narrated to me that whenever he would go home to his province, his grandfather would be waiting at the porch of the house and upon seeing him would say, "I have been waiting for you to come!" Apparently, the grandfather had been sending him mental messages for him to come home and see him.

ETHERIC DOUBLE

The apartment we occupied in Bangkal, Makati City was owned by Mr. Florencio Cruz and Mrs. Anastacia Legisma, both retired government employees. The man had worked for the Central Bank while the woman was formerly an elementary school teacher. My sisters and I occupied the ground floor of the house while the old couple lived upstairs.

The old man's health deteriorated much faster than the old woman after he retired from work in spite of his working on his beautiful garden daily. Towards the latter part of 1988, he hardly goes down to work in the garden. His legs were swollen and he found it quite difficult to walk especially to negotiate the long stairwell to and from the second floor of the house which they occupy.

I got a grant from the Furniture Industry Research Association of Europe as a furniture exporter. The grant for that year was given to eight furniture manufacturer-exporters and included free consultancy on production, product design and marketing. Since the project was ASEAN-wide, (Association of South East Asian Nations), FIRA took a big selling space in High Point, North Carolina, the center of furniture manufacturing and distribution in the United States so that its grantees can experience actual selling in big distribution centers. As an added bonus, the grantees were invited to visit the FIRA offices and testing centers in London.

The market week in High Point was towards the end of October 1988. A couple of nights before I left for the United States, I was soundly sleeping on a specially made bamboo bed when I felt like urinating. The feeling woke me up and as I turned sideways to get up towards my left, I saw lying beside me the green transparent shape of a person. I opened my eyes wide in disbelief but I did not feel afraid, anymore. In fact the phenomenon even excited me. I closely took a look at the reclining figure as I slowly got up, went over it and stood up. Then I examined it again while standing on my feet. It was lying so serenely and it was shaped exactly as the terra cotta priest, which I painted white, by the door of the apartment.

However, deep within my mind, I kept thinking of the sick old man upstairs. Could it be his "etheric double" that separates from his physical body at night while he sleeps so that it can lie beside me? I remembered the talks I had with Ka Nitoy wherein he said that old people like children very much because the children can easily absorb energy from the sun, energy which are stored in their etheric doubles and that by getting near to children, old folks can partake of the energy from those children without either of them consciously being aware of what takes place. He added that the etheric double of old people float around at night while they sleep and go near young people in order to absorb energy from them. That was the reason why some children in the company of several old people easily get sick because their energy is drained.

I remembered the advice of Ka Nitoy on what to do in such cases so after relieving myself at the comfort room, I took a basin half-filled with water. The transparent figure was no longer there when I returned with the basin of water. Just the same, I placed it on the floor near my bamboo bed. That water was intended to prevent the ethic double from getting near me, water being the antidote according to Ka Nitoy.

The following night, I again placed a basin half-filled with water near my bed. I went to bed at around ten in the evening. Somehow, I woke up at around two in the morning. No transparent figure was lying beside me. I looked down on the floor; the basin was still there. I went back to sleep and got up at four to prepare for my long plane trip to the United States.

The grantees from the Philippines were expected at a specified date to be in London. I went to the United States a few days earlier to be with my parents and sisters who live in California. From California, I took a flight to London and came back to the United States three days later via New York en route to High Point in time for the Market Week.

I came back to the Philippines in early November after passing by San Francisco to visit some relatives and friends. I was surprised to see my sister and her husband at the San Francisco airport when I arrived. It turned out that they traveled by van from Los Angeles to San Francisco to time their visit with my arrival there.

After a few days stay in that city, I went back to the Philippines. On arrival, I found out that Mr. Cruz, my landlord had died shortly after I left for the United States.

Was my suspicion that his **etheric double**'s inability to get energy from me while I was asleep hastened his death true?

BAFFLING REMITTANCE

FIRA, acronym for Furniture Industry Research Association of Europe with headquarters near London, England sponsored my trip to High Point, North Carolina in the United States of America. That was in 1988.

I established Amaranth Design Showcase, a furniture designing and exporting business, in December of 1984. Amaranth was able to start actual exporting in mid 1986 after joining a trade show in which one of the furniture it exhibited won a "Katha Award" for excellence in furniture design. Ten products from ten manufacturers out of 82 participants were given the award.

The Design Center of the Philippines, one of the sponsoring agencies gave me the cash prize of five thousand pesos but the winners were not given the plaques of recognition because it had to be signed by the President of the Philippines. Unfortunately, the first People Power Revolution just transpired the week before the international trade show. The newly installed President, Mrs. Corazon Aquino was so busy attending to myriads of things that they don't want to bother her with the signing of the plaques. There were press releases, nevertheless, proclaiming the winners in the year's "Katha Awards".

In 1987, in partnership with an Australian furniture buyer and some Filipino friends, we acquired a company called Noir et Blanc Corporation. I was elected president of the corporation tasked with the day-to-day operations of the firm as well as product design and Madeleine Beattie, elected chairman was tasked to handle export marketing.

Noir et Blanc Corporation was eventually chosen among several applicants to the ASEAN Consultancy Program of FIRA. Aside from providing free consultancy services in the areas of production, quality control, design and marketing, free display space and free air fare for one representative of each of the chosen firms was also given by FIRA.

It was decided that I should represent our firm in High Point, North Carolina but Madeleine will also go at her own expense. Our initial shipment of wooden components to a New York buyer showed some quality problems and Madeleine wanted me to talk to the owner of A.S.I.F., Mr. Mark Goldsmith of New York whose family owns a big business engaged in the manufacture of display mannequins.

Our company was really a small one and we did not put in any cash funds because our plan was to avail of bank financing once orders come in.

Therefore, joining the FIRA project was a "bahala na" attitude on my part, meaning, "come what may" God will take care of the rest. And so He did!

Fifteen days before the scheduled departure for the United States, I still did not have enough funds for my plane fare, hotel and food expenses. Though FIRA promised to shoulder our plane fare tickets, they advised the representatives that their respective firms had to shell out the money first then they will reimburse later when we submit the used tickets.

Actually, it was all right if I could not go, Madeleine would be there anyway. By that time our furniture samples had already been shipped together with the samples of the other participants.

Unexpectedly, I received a call from one of my banks, the Bank of the Philippine Islands, oldest existing bank in the country. I was told that there was a remittance for me from Australia and New Zealand Bank. I was surprised because I was not expecting any remittance from Australia since all orders had been shipped out already. I told the bank staff to check with ANZ Bank if they have the right addressee because I know I was not the proper recipient. In the meantime I would check with Madeleine if she had sent any money to me.

The bank called me again to say that the funds remitted were really intended for my account. I told them I could not accept the funds because it did not belong to me. I have already asked Madeleine if she sent any money and she said she has no recollection of any recent remittance. Much as I refuse to accept the funds, the bank firmly said they could not do anything but credit my account for the funds as instructed by their counterpart bank.

My funding problem was no more. The funds were enough to buy me a round trip plane ticket and would leave extra for my lodging and food while on travel. **It must be God's answer to my need.**

In California

I left for the United States via NorthWest Airlines early October. The Furniture Show would be on the third week of October. Flight from Manila to Japan took four hours. I had to deplane for the connecting flight to Los Angeles in California. Though I still had to go to London, I opted to go there via the United States instead of via Europe because my mother and my sister Girlie were then living in California near Los Angeles. One of my nieces would be having her 7th birthday on the 8th of October.

My parents were there at the Los Angeles Airport together with Girlie, my sister and Bobby, her husband. Bobby immigrated to the United States in the late seventies. He married my sister Girlie in 1981 in Manila and as soon as he got back to the mainland, he petitioned for my sister. Eventually, my mother went there also to take care of Girlie's children. That was after she retired early from teaching as an option.

It was my first trip to the United States and the long trip took something like 16 hours from Japan to the mainland. It was beautiful up there over the clouds. Though one can faintly hear the sound of the jet engines of the plane, when one looks outside the window, it was as if the plane was not moving at all. It was as if it was suspended in the sky.

My sister and her husband were able to buy a beautiful house in Walnut County perched high up on a hill. They assigned me to the room overlooking a small overhang of a terrace and furnished it with a pull out sofa-bed. Eventually, they would refer to it as "Junior's Room". My mother sleeps with the three little girls, Girlie's children. The couple sleeps in the big master's bedroom.

On my second day, somebody called by the name of Susan Reyes. I wondered who she was but she was indeed looking for me. She introduced herself as the sister of Pete Reyes, Jr., one of my close friends in Manila. It turned out that Pete called his sister who was then living in Los Angeles and requested her to show me around the Hollywood area. She came for me in her bantam car dressed casually in pants and polo shirt with a jacket on top. My mother was smiling because in the Philippines it was usually the guys who fetch the girls for a spin in their car. But I was in America and they do things differently over there.

Susan was very pleasant to talk to. She drove very fast that I felt like falling off my seat in spite of the seat belt whenever we would come onto a curb.

She brought me to the Observatory, near the giant Hollywood sign; we drove through the Sunset Boulevard; had dinner at the Spaghetti Factory, a restaurant specializing in spaghettis; drove around the Hollywood area; had coffee at El Figaro, where we had to wait for a seat; finally she brought me to a shop where they sell all kinds of sex books, tapes, and gadgets. It was already 1:00 a.m. by then and Los Angeles was very much alive.

It was around 2:30 a.m. when she brought me back to my sister's house and I thanked her profusely for the wonderful evening. That was the first and last time I saw her. I heard from her brother in Manila that she studied physical therapy and moved over to Miami. I did not ask what kind of work she had in Los Angeles but later; her brother told me that she was the editor of the Penthouse Magazine but using an assumed American name.

She was inviting me to go with her to Malibu the following day, Saturday but my mother and sister advised me against it, saying that Malibu is quite far and we won't be able to get back on the same day in time for the birthday party. So I refused the invitation.

Some close relatives living in Mountain View near San Francisco came for the birthday party. They had just bought a camper van and wanted to try it on a long drive. San Francisco to L.A. usually takes eight hours by land.

Many other visitors came, mostly relatives of Bobby and office mates of Girlie. After mingling with the guests for several hours, I had to turn in at around 9:30 p.m. because I could not open my sleepy eyes anymore. I found it difficult to adjust to the time in America, which was the complete opposite of the time in Manila so that I felt sleepy most of the time.

Sunday, we started early for Disneyland, the famous land of wonders.

The whole family went to Disneyland except for my father who opted to stay at home. I better not detail what we have seen over there because most people are familiar with the place. The only thing I noticed was its huge parking area for vehicles and a tall hotel near the entrance to the amusement area. My mother used to work at another hotel just across the Disneyland Hotel while my father worked for just a week at Disneyland's parking booth. He did not last with that job because his nose was bleeding due to the cold weather. In any case, when he retired from his teaching job as an elementary school principal, he decided he should not do any work anymore, even at home.

It was already late at night when we got back to my sister's home. We went to bed as soon as we got there because I had to fly to London the following day. Though it was a Monday, I understand that my sister and her husband took several days off from their offices to attend to my visit.

FLATTERIES IN LONDON

I did not notify our host, FIRA with the details of my flight so that I did not expect anyone to fetch me at the Heathrow Airport. It was good that when I changed some currencies to pounds, I saw a sign that the train station is located at the basement of the airport. The train would bring me to central London. I asked around what station I should get down to that would be nearest the Tower Hotel where the participants from Asia were booked. The train ride was about 30 minutes and as it neared the city, the train gradually entered the tunnel, hence the term "underground" when referring to the train stations. I usually mistook the term for "underpass" which referred to a pedestrian passage.

I had to take three flights of escalators before I came upon the street level. My baggage was heavy and I seemed to have lost my sense of direction so that after walking a block, I flagged down a taxi. The taxi driver took me in and asked where I wanted to go. I asked him if he knew where Tower Hotel was and he said yes. I loaded my bags and went inside the taxi. He made a turn on the next street and there we were at the hotel. The billing did not even hit one pound. In my embarrassment, I gave the driver two pounds.

The following morning, somebody from FIRA called on me. We had to go to their office outside of London for the briefing and tour of the testing facilities. We rode a small bus together with the ASEAN participants to the program, namely from Malaysia, Singapore, Indonesia, Brunei, Thailand and the Philippines. I was told that had I faxed to them the details of my flight, they would have sent somebody to fetch me at the airport. I also learned that I missed the dinner tendered for the participants the previous evening. To think that I had to shell out fifteen pounds for my dinner of roasted lamb that evening in the hotel restaurant.

I was the only Filipino in the group who took the bus that morning. Apparently, they did not have any information if the other Filipino participants will still pass by London. We had a briefing at their office about what FIRA does and then we were given a short tour of the facilities.

We were loaded again in the bus for lunch in an English restaurant. As we were about to park, a taxi pulled in and a Filipino got off. His name is Rupert Cruz, manufacturer of heavily carved wooden furniture and architectural components from Pampanga province. He was so glad to see me. He said that he had wanted to talk to me except that he could not find me in Manila. I was flattered because I did not think that a gentleman of his stature knew who I was.

We were introduced to the other ASEAN participants during lunch. I happened to sit across the office secretary of FIRA. I forgot her name but she was the one in-charge of all communications regarding the project. She whispered to me that, in all honesty, her favorite among the products presented for evaluation was my bone-inlaid wooden jewelry case. Another flattery for me that day.

We were brought back to the hotel late in the afternoon. We were free to go the succeeding days, to go to America. I stayed for a couple of days more.

Rupert told me that he would stay for only a day more as he had to fly to Germany for a couple of days. The following day, we met at the hotel lobby so we can walk around the vicinity of the hotel and scout around for books, art books or furniture books. We passed by the Tower Bridge, the famous drawbridge across the River Thames.

There were quite a number of bookstores with new stocks and we bought what interested us. We had simple meals in small restaurants nearby. The following day, Rupert left for Germany to see a buyer.

On my third day in London, I explored the city by myself. I bought a ticket to be able to explore the Tower Bridge from end to end; took the red double decker bus to Victoria Station; went to Hyde Park and saw the boat races. By the way, when I was bound for London from Los Angeles, I had a wish to see the Rotunda where they shot a scene for the film "Oliver"; where a lady was singing," Who will buy my beautiful roses, who will buy this wonderful feeling?" As I was walking a quiet neighborhood, I suddenly came upon the semi-circular apartment row where they shot the scene. I could not believe I would see it by mere chance!

I was exhausted when I got back to the hotel that evening. I placed a call to New York to find out if any of my cousins will see me at the airport. The following day, I went down the tube to take the train to Heathrow Airport.

A Night In New York

I had a vivid dream several days before I left for the United States. In the dream I felt I was seated on a chair before a small rectangular table. There was a cup of coffee before me, which I must be drinking. A table lamp illumined the room and gave one such a cozy feeling. It was very dark outside as can be seen through the glass window, being nighttime. It also seemed very cold outside. I looked around the room from where I was. Not so far away, I saw by the sink a beautiful woman washing the dishes. She was saying something but I could not hear her voice. I do know, however, that she was talking to me. The dream was very short yet very vivid.

In New York's La Guardia Airport, two of my cousins were waiting for me when I got there. There was Josie and her brother Ric Mendoza, my second cousins who have since relocated in New York from Manila. When I was in high school, I used to spend my Sundays with their family without fail.

Josie was already separated from her husband after three years of living together. I did see her husband one time in the Philippines. Ric who was inseparable with his brother Manuel (nicknamed Boy) was also my playmate. They were the ones who used to lend me their toys whenever I go to their place in spite of the fact that I was quite older than they were. From the moment I stepped into college I seldom visited them because my university was quite far from where they live in Manila.

It was only in New York that I learned Ric had gotten married but I did not know whom he married. It seemed to me that he was the playboy type between the two brothers. Manuel had also gotten married and settled in California but I haven't met him there. The rest of their siblings, Rene, Tita, Arsenia, Roland and Jet remained in the Philippines.

From the airport, we proceeded to the apartment of Lita, their sister, who used to work with Philippine Airlines. They were telling me that Lita was operating a sausage business; that she has a lovely daughter; that she was about to separate from her husband, too.

We had supper at Lita's place. They were asking me if I wanted to go to the disco in New York City but I declined because I was tired. Besides, I don't want them to miss their offices the following day.

After dinner, we proceeded to Josie's apartment. She lived there with Ric and his wife. Lita and her daughter came with us to sleep with Josie. Lita used to live with them when she was not yet married. The apartment was at the third floor of the structure so we had a hard time bringing up my heavy stuff. It was located somewhere in Queens. Josie prepared the sofa-bed in the living room so I can occupy it for the night then all of us went to bed except for Ric who went out to fetch his wife from the office.

I was trying to read a flyer or something and did not notice that I fell asleep with the light on. I woke up at around 4:00 a.m.. I heard somebody moving in the kitchen. It must be Josie, I thought. I stood up and went to the toilet to take a leak. It was dark outside but the light from the living room lamp was lighting the whole room except for some areas where the walls cast dark shadows. The kitchen was in fact half lighted and half dark. From the toilet, I sat on one of the chairs by the dining table. There was a coffee mug with some hot coffee on the table.

"I'm having coffee, would you like some?" I heard a sweet voice say from the dark corner of the room by the drain. I looked at the direction of the voice and from the dark, I saw the blurred image of a woman. I said," Yes, I could use some." She took a cup from the cabinet, filled it with hot water and stepped out of the dark towards me. She was so beautiful in the light and so feminine inside her robe. She introduced herself to be the wife of Ric then pointed to the bottles of instant coffee, sugar and cream to me. I prepared my coffee the way I wanted it and had some short conversation with Ric's wife. I couldn't recall anymore her name but she worked as secretary in the embassy of an African State, probably Senegal.

As I was sipping my coffee, it dawned on me that the scene was very familiar. Oh yes, I remembered the dream of several weeks earlier. Is that what the French refer to as déjà vu?

We went back to bed after consuming the coffee. The following morning I did not see her or Ric anymore. They had gone to office. Lita and her daughter were also gone. Josie offered to show me around downtown New York. We reached the city proper by bus at around ten o'clock so the people of New York and its environs were already inside the tall buildings. She showed me the St. Patrick Cathedral, the Empire State building, the Rockefeller Foundation building and the Donald Trump building. We had a sandwich lunch then went back to the apartment in Queens. I had to catch my flight to North Carolina with connecting flight in Atlanta.

Shortly after we got back to the apartment, Ric arrived in his BMW car. We loaded my suitcase and my backpack into the car and got in. We were running a little late so when we were almost at the airport, my cousin Josie told me not to react when she talks to the guard by the airport entrance.

I was surprised when she said, "Can we just park here at the shoulder for a short while, the ambassador is taking a flight and we don't want him to miss his flight?" The black security guard did not object so Ric parked the car near the entrance. Josie went in with me and surprisingly, Rupert Cruz was there at the waiting area. It turned out that we had booked for the same flight. It was a happy coincidence too that Josie knew him quite well from the stories a close friend so they had quite a conversation at the airport while we were waiting for boarding call.

I passed by New York for one and a half day only, yet in must be significant because though I only had a few minutes of conversation with Ric's wife, I saw that scene in my dream beforehand. Could it be that she was someone I knew in a past life?

TO SUMMARIZE

Spiritual Teachers say that space, time and self are but illusions.

That contrary to our usual beliefs, space or what we perceive to be the distance between two points is not empty but actually completely solid. The objects seen in space like people, trees, planets, etc. are holes.

For man, the microcosm there is past, present and future but from the point of view of the macrocosm or God, there is no time at all. The only Reality is Now. They say that God sees the whole event from beginning to end. They also say that before a spirit is reincarnated, he will be shown the panorama of his life and will be allowed to assume a body of flesh, a new garment, only if he agrees to what is in store for him.

That probably explains why whenever I would meet a vehicular accident, I would usually feel uneasy, uncomfortable and bothered that I might meet an accident two or three days before the actual incident occurs. This kind of feeling happened maybe three or four times. On the day of the accident, however, the feeling of uneasiness about the lurking danger would dissipate so that I would not be cautious of my driving on the day of the accident.

Is there a "self"?

When the body of young Hector tumbled down the bamboo stairs, the body cried but the seer did not feel any pain because it was detached from the body. When the seer is inside the body, it will feel every sensation that the body feels if it is aware or conscious. However, when it is unconscious as when it loses consciousness, it will not sense anything that the body will feel. Like when I temporarily lost consciousness when at 18 years of age I had mumps. I fell to the ground but did not feel any pain because consciousness left the body.

Sages say that "life is but a dream" or imagination of God. When we dream or imagine, we create nothing more than mind stuff. When God imagines, things come into existence but just the same the objects we see are the mind stuff of God.

About The Book

If there's one thing that the author wants, it is to be able to share his psychic experiences with as many people as possible. However, cognizant of the fact that not all peoples will be curious on his subject, he decided to write these into a book for anybody interested to read.

He narrated here some of his unusual experiences spanning a period of fifty years. Sometimes they did not seem logically explainable, sometimes they were doubtful, sometimes hair-raising, sometimes wonderful.

In many instances, he had recurring dreams, so vivid that they almost seem real. At a later time, he would be a witness to the scenery or the situation he saw in his dreams. At first, he doubted his recollections so he tried to list down his dreams of unusual places or events just so he can be sure when it has happened that indeed, he dreamt about it. The French have a term for it, déjà vu, isn't it?

He had not experienced seeing dead people as ghosts, but he was sure he heard something to convince him that they are still very much around.

These are some of the experiences he narrated, which you could have experienced yourself.

Author's Biography

Hector Fernandez is a CPA and an MBA degree.holder.

He was third placer in the 1965 Manila Archdiocese-wide essay-writing contest.

He won a "Katha Award" for excellence in furniture design in 1986.

Hector currently works with PNOC.

Sundays he anchors a radio program entitled, "Learnings from Life's Lessons".

www.ingramcontent.com/pod-product-compliance
Lightning Source LLC
Chambersburg PA
CBHW031233280526
45784CB00004B/1559